The Wisdom of Love

The Wisdom of Love

Alain Finkielkraut

La sagesse de l'amour

Translated by Kevin O'Neill
and David Suchoff

University of Nebraska Press

Lincoln & London

Publication of this translation
was assisted by a grant
from the French Ministry of Culture.

⊜ The paper in this book meets the minimum requirements of American National Standard
for Information Sciences — Permanence of Paper for
Printed Library Materials, ANSI z39.48-1984.

Library of Congress Cataloging in Publication Data
Finkielkraut, Alain.
[Sagesse de l'amour. English] The wisdom of love =
(La sagesse de l'amour) / Alain Finkielkraut :
translated by Kevin O'Neill and David Suchoff.
p.   cm. – (Texts and contexts: v. 20)
Includes bibliographical references and index.
ISBN 0-8032-1991-1
1. Civilization, Modern – 1950– 2. Civilization.
Modern — Philosophy. 3. Love. 4. Multi-
culturalism. 5. Conservatism.
6. Liberalism. I. Series.
CB428.F5713 1997 306'.01–dc20
96-9823 CIP

For Sylvie Topaloff

Contents

Introduction by David Suchoff

To speak of love, as Alain Finkielkraut does in this book, evokes a conservative return to values, seemingly at odds with the critical project of modernity. But *The Wisdom of Love* is a deceptively titled work. Originally published in 1984 by a major French intellectual who had already authored a critique of American conservatism as well as a book on Jewish identity, and who would go on to write an iconoclastic work on the culture wars, this book aims to unsettle the easy distinction between cultural liberalism and conservatism that continues to shape contemporary debate. It was written as the Marxist project lost credibility with the Western left and as liberalism was challenged by the claims of cultural difference; its historical moment and its grounding in the ethical thought of Emmanuel Lévinas make it a unique rethinking of love as a critical ground for social thought. The wisdom Finkielkraut offers here is no rehash of traditional pieties but a way of thinking about the relationship between minority and majority culture in an increasingly multicultural age. *The Wisdom of Love* thus bears on two topics crucial to contemporary cultural politics: the problem of reconciling the right to cultural difference with the demands of community, and how the thought of Lévinas sketches a new position—committed to universalism but also to preserving the particularism of Jewish and other minority cultures—in our multicultural debates.

FINKIELKRAUT AND THE CULTURE WARS

Finkielkraut differs sharply from the American cultural conservatives in his views on the relation between minority and majority cultures. *The Wisdom of Love* supports neither the nostalgic, universalist traditionalism represented by E. D. Hirsch or William Bennett nor the partisanship for the ethnic or racial Other that is often labeled "politically correct" by its opponents. Rather than view multicultural diversity as antithetical to Western ideals or as a destructive challenge to cultural tradition, Finkielkraut sees cultural difference as the rightful claim that the Other makes to be included, as different, within the tradition of universal rights. This universalism led Finkielkraut to sometimes hyperbolic attacks on the multicultural movement in a subsequent book, *The Defeat of the Mind*.[1] But American readers would be mistaken to ally Finkielkraut with American opponents of multiculturalism. To make the point quite bluntly, *The Wisdom of Love* is far more concerned with preserving the Other's difference than is American neoconservatism, which tends to see multiculturalism as a threat leading to "The Decomposition of America" and the fracturing of our universal American values.[2] Finkielkraut's universalism, by contrast, grounds itself in Emmanuel Lévinas's theory of the Other, whose anti-assimilationist roots in Jewish sources make the preservation of the Other's difference the central impulse of his thought.

The Other's claim for inclusion, Finkielkraut argues here, is a rightful claim to justice. The West began to bemoan its loss of universal concepts, he suggests, at precisely the historical moment that non-Western cultures began to claim their share of them: that is, when "Other" cultures called into question the European "center" and its stable sense of self as the decolonization movement took hold in the 1950s. In American cultural debate, this decentering has often been blamed on "theory" and its supposedly baneful effect on the Academy, for the loss of great authors or for the loss of a sure sense of the universal truths of Western culture. Finkielkraut, on the other hand, might be said to agree with W. E. B. Du Bois's famous dictum, pronounced in *The Souls of Black Folk,* that "the problem of the Twentieth Century is the problem of the color-line."[3] The claims of the Other must be addressed, Finkielkraut argues here, but only in the spirit of Du Bois or the cultural Zionist Achad Ha-am: with a critical view of any racial or ethnic essentialism.

How can one love the Other without essentializing, or thereby reducing, Otherness? The question of "love" posed in this book is the pressing question faced by social thought in the postcolonial age. Through a clear exposition of Lévinas's notoriously rich and difficult thought, using examples from Proust, Henry James, and others, Finkielkraut shows how love of others is both a romantic and a profoundly ethical and political question. How, *The Wisdom of Love* asks us to consider, can one—or one's culture—encounter and value Otherness without fetishizing, reducing, or even destroying it in love's name? All the crucial issues faced in the twentieth century, this book reminds us in its preface, bring us to speak of love.

Finkielkraut's answer has been a critical return to liberalism, through a rethinking of its assimilationist tradition. Like many of the "new *philosophes,*" the post-Marxist group of French intellectuals who have sought to theorize liberal democracy anew since the 1980s, Finkielkraut has been disappointed by Marxism's quest for the "other" who explains the dialectic of world history.[4] In *The Wisdom of Love,* Finkielkraut argues that the "other" is reduced when the particularity of the ethnic self—or the erotic object—is elevated to become a fixed essence. Love's wisdom, as Finkielkraut develops it from Lévinas's thought, means keeping the question of the Other open. This book's critique of a left in decline, however, represented by the disastrous brutality of Europe's Red Brigade of the 1980s, should not be confused with a merely rightward turn. For Finkielkraut, "Love" does not mean selfless moralism and universal "knowledge," as some cultural conservatives recommend, but the acceptance of the Other's likeness and right to exist within the Western tradition as irreducibly different. *The Wisdom of Love* demands respect for ethnic and racial particularity as a difference opposed to any totalizing ideological, national, or ethnic scheme.

One contribution of *The Wisdom of Love* is therefore its critique of the logic that stands behind liberal versions of multiculturalism. That critique is offered by a writer committed to a central European tradition that knows firsthand the falsity of liberal promises of cultural inclusion. European Jews, as Finkielkraut noted in *The Imaginary Jew,* "fell in love with the Rights of Man," only to discover the price of inclusion to be self-hatred and a hatred of the Other that refused to subside. Multicultural inclusion, for Finkielkraut, represents the postmodern form of liberal inclusivity, now based on the praise of and pride in difference rather than assimilation. *The Wisdom of Love,* however, suspects this new inclusiveness: for as humanism takes the Other, as different, into its loving embrace, this liberal center also patronizes the objects of its "acceptance," offering what in American parlance might sound like the "victim" status that right-leaning cultural critics on the center and right have often decried. "Since the society you have internalized is guilty," Finkielkraut writes, "you are innocent: this sums up the credo of modern humanism." What must be noticed here is the difference between Finkielkraut's critique of liberal humanism and right-wing American variants of this theme. Finkielkraut does not rail against the "culture of victimization," a term often used in the American context as a kind of "blacklash" to decry the advances women and minorities have made.[5] *The Wisdom of Love* instead argues against the trivialization and patronage of the Other that is still able to present itself as "protecting" minorities and their cultural difference, but that ends up denying them the universal human rights enjoyed by members of the majority.

The project of liberating cultural difference, Finkielkraut points out incisively, began to join hands in the 1980s with a viewpoint that conceived the West and its tradition as an overwhelming and totalizing source of social control. In the general press, this point of view was simplified as the "politically correct" view that the Western tradition was strictly a source of repression. In late cold-war America, such positions were often called "containment" arguments and were launched specifically against the idea of America's liberal "consensus" to correct its narrow view of the role of minorities in American history and culture or to indicate the false promises of social justice that American liberalism had made. American proponents of multiculturalism or liberal centrism, in other words, have carried on their arguments against the cultural right and its exclusion or neglect of minority cultures. *The Wisdom of Love,* by contrast, carries out its debate with the excesses of France's left, whose postmodern and adolescent identification with Otherness Finkielkraut would later come to parody in the chapter entitled "We Are the World, We Are the Children" in *The Defeat of the Mind.*[6] What worries Finkielkraut in this book is the absence of any position between the "love" for the Other, which trivializes, patronizes, or manufactures cultural difference, and repression of the Other, the conservative claim for a cultural universality that leaves the Other unheard. In Lévinas's terms, the Other makes a claim on us based on likeness, while remaining different to the categories we apply. Sustaining this tension, for Finkielkraut, defines the crucial task of the cultural centrism, given the failures of universalist liberalism to recognize the claims of cultural difference in the past.

Introduction by David Suchoff

Rather than dissect the right, *The Wisdom of Love* therefore invests much of its energy in detailing the limitations of liberal humanism, for it is a book concerned with constructing the tradition of republican universalism anew. European recognition of this effort came in the Prix Européen de l'Essai Charles Veillon, which was awarded to this book in 1984. Accepting that prize, Finkielkraut made quite clear his critique of universalist notions of a culture that might underlie a new civic republicanism. There he defined *culture*—perhaps the most crucial, if inadequately debated, term in contemporary intellectual discussion—as that which expresses the "life of a people, group, or collectivity."[7] This part of his speech clearly points to his criticism of that progressive liberalism that would swallow the other's cultural difference. *The Wisdom of Love* makes this clear in its witty critique of Homais, the idiotic progressive of *Madame Bovary*. In a discussion that relies on Sartre but that also remains a cutting critique of him, Finkielkraut shows how the "revolutionary," progressive thinker cancels the particularity of the Other he would save. By elevating difference into a "universal" value, the progressive creates a new dogma, canceling the challenging claim of the Other. Liberal patronage, Finkielkraut shows, cancels the cultural particularity of the Other unconsciously, achieving the avowed program of the conservative through more "benevolent" means.

Finkielkraut, however, also offers strident criticism of any support for cultural difference that limits the universal freedoms promised by the liberal tradition. "The Other," *The Wisdom of Love* argues, "is not freed by granting him a unique, even a prestigious, essence." This position relies philosophically on Lévinas, whose phenomenological ethics argues powerfully against reducing the irreducibly different "face" (*visage*) of the Other and its ethical challenge into a categorically abstract otherness. Here, Finkielkraut's opposition to Moslem women being permitted to wear the foulard or head covering in French schools—or Jewish students the *kipa* or skullcap—provides a controversial case in which *The Wisdom of Love* and Finkielkraut's role as a prominent public intellectual meet. Schooled in diversity and lacking the tradition of an established church, an American audience might well consider such French universalism as threatening a right to difference that most Americans take for granted. It is a position that certainly indicates the depths, and some would say the limits, of the position of *The Wisdom of Love* in cultural practice.

Yet the position cannot be fairly evaluated unless the critical value of such universalism is seen. It is "a strange antiracism," as Finkielkraut put it during the controversy, "that reduces the Jew to Judaism, the Moslem to Islam, the black to Black is beautiful, which, in a general way, says every individual possesses no being but that of the species."[8] A critical cultural universalism, as Finkielkraut has suggested elsewhere, makes critical use of universal values to criticize the limitations of religious, national, ethnic, or racial identity. It is this tension between universal and particular forms of cultural identity that marks this book's essays and the critique of liberalism they provide. "Culture," as Finkielkraut's full definition put it in his prize-acceptance speech, "and perhaps even European culture," consists of that which expresses "the life of a people, group, or collectivity, but which escapes the limits of collective being."[9]

"Love" for Finkielkraut thus becomes a critical concept that splits the camps in the contemporary culture wars that have taken sides across this divide. *The Wisdom of Love* bears no resemblance to the implicit ethnocentrism of William Bennett's *The Book of Virtues* (1993): Finkielkraut's universalism aims at fracturing the hold of cultural power over the individual, rather than endorsing adherence to dominant pieties in virtue's name. Love's wisdom, on the contrary, defends against the Other's premature absorption into majority culture, cautioning against submerging the Other's ethical demands in universal schemes of progress or cultural norms. This critical universalism, hostile to the idea of cultural assimilation, has attracted its critics on the left, particularly where Jewish cultural sources and experience contribute to multicultural thought. Paul Gilroy, for instance, fears that Lévinas's comments on Jewish suffering claim too much authentic specificity for Jewish culture, at the expense of other minority cultures, especially where the Holocaust is concerned.[10] Finkielkraut's use of Lévinas adheres neither to the easy universalism of American neoconservatives nor to those sections of the cultural left critical of Jewish claims to cultural difference. The difficulty one has placing Finkielkraut springs from the novelty of his use of Lévinas and Jewish sources within the multicultural debate.

A JEWISH POSITION IN THE MULTICULTURAL DEBATE?

Finkielkraut's differential model of cultural identity—combining a commitment to universal values kept in skeptical check by the claims of cultural difference—is not the only contemporary position to depend on Jewish sources in general, and Emmanuel Lévinas in particular. Jacques Derrida's development of deconstruction, which argues for the ineffaceability of difference in textual terms, was also formed in dialogue with the ethical theory formulated by Lévinas, which strives to preserve the infinite possibilities of the Other from false totalization.[11] The double structure of Lévinas's work reflects this dual commitment to preservation of Jewish particularity within the larger culture of the West. Steeped in the Western philosophical tradition, Lévinas is also an expositor and renewer of the tradition of Central

European Jewish thought.[12] Finkielkraut studied intensively with Lévinas; readers interested in Lévinas's Jewish sources, and Finkielkraut as a "disciple" of their teachings, will benefit from Judith Friedlander's work, which provides a superb introduction to Lévinas as a whole.[13]

But the idea of Finkielkraut's "discipleship" needs to be qualified by an important difference between the two thinkers. The signal contribution of *The Wisdom of Love* is to bring Lévinas's concept of the Other—and the Jewish sources that sustain it—into critical tension with the larger contemporary debate on multiculturalism. Lévinas, by contrast, as Jill Robbins and others have pointed out, has taken great pains to separate his work on Jewish material from his central philosophic concerns.[14] His contributions in both areas have been considerable. Lévinas wrote the first major philosophic treatment of Husserl, crucial to the development of Sartre's thought, and authored two landmark philosophic works, *Otherwise Than Being, or Beyond Essence* and *Totality and Infinity*, "a bracing tract on the open-endedness of human possibility," in George Steiner's words, and a powerful argument for the utopian ineffaceability of cultural difference.[15] His essays on Jewish cultural and political questions, collected in the volume *Difficult Liberty*, and his explications of the Talmud, a yearly event in France, have influenced the study and renewal of Jewish intellectual life in France and beyond. Still, the separation remains. While scholars appreciate the connections between Lévinas's philosophical *oeuvre* and his grounding in classics of central European Jewish thought like Franz Rosenzweig's *Star of Redemption*—a work crucial to Walter Benjamin as well—Lévinas himself has held the two universes of discourse apart.

The Wisdom of Love, by contrast, brings the problems of multicultural identity into direct and critical contact with the Jewish historical experience of difference in the West. A crucial case in point is Finkielkraut's use of the Dreyfus affair.[16] Today, as Finkielkraut went to hyperbolic lengths to point out in *The Defeat of the Mind,* thinkers on the cultural left value difference above all as a criterion for cultural authenticity and validity. Historically, however, defining a citizen as culturally different was a position that belonged to the right. Finkielkraut discusses "The Ethnic Nose" to remind us that French conservatives like Barrès projected Dreyfus as a cultural foreigner in order to ground their right-wing sense that the cultural center possessed an organic validity. Freedom, Finkielkraut reminds us, consists in the right to assert one's cultural difference, as well as one's identity with the dominant culture, and asks us to balance today's "slogans celebrating difference," which remains part of multiculturalism's claim to cultural justice, with the emancipatory ideal of liberal citizenship in the West, whose ideals refused to lock the individual within the bounds cast by race and ethnicity.[17]

The Dreyfus case and its imprisoning figuration of Jewish ethnicity allow Finkielkraut to offer a larger analysis of hatred, ever more pertinent as liberal political sentiment in Europe and the United States turns increasingly hostile to immigrant Others. Hatred of the Other, Finkielkraut shows us, results not so much from our rejection of difference but from our recognition of the Other's identity with us and from our rejection of the call for universal justice that presents itself in culturally specific forms. Talk-show host Rush Limbaugh, who decries liberal compassion with hateful vehemence, makes the same point: rejection of the Other results not from contempt for difference but fear of the human similarity that obligates us to those who retain their difference. Attacks on multiculturalism also fit the pattern Finkielkraut sketches here: the Other is hated for his identity to the culture we prize as "ours." The liberalism that sees society at fault for all social ills must be corrected, Finkielkraut argues, not to abolish concern for the other as crippling "welfare" but to assure that the culturally different retain their cultural specificity and individual agency within the public sphere.

Like Lévinas, Finkielkraut reads Jewish historical experience and culture for its universal contributions to our public culture, breaking with the tradition of Jewish assimilation. Yet *The Wisdom of Love* envisions that public sphere outside the sphere of traditional religion. Finkielkraut criticizes liberal humanism, however, for abandoning the ethical tradition of religion, thereby robbing the Other of the individual specificity that makes action possible. Enlightenment humanism, Finkielkraut argues, separated man from religion, only to place the individual under the spell of the social.

Lévinas, as *The Wisdom of Love* expounds him, argues once again for individual ethical autonomy, in a reading of the Jewish tradition that brings it closer to what is normally understood as atheism. It is not God who speaks in Lévinas but the face of the Other, which demands justice and recognition. Finkielkraut uses Lévinas to trace the ground between a liberalism, or Marxism, that collapses the Other into the social and thus silences cultural agency and specificity of the individual, and a respect for the Other that is grounded in religious thought but that refuses to deify, or reify, the ethical demand. Much of Judaism, Finkielkraut reminds us, is loath to speak of the Supreme Being, since such talk—like the liberalism he decries—might universalize the ethical demand to know the Other, a universal demand that can only be addressed in concrete, specific instances in the world.

Finkielkraut's analysis of passion's wisdom suggests that the same messianic hope inheres in the difference and frustration that define romantic love. For Lévinas, the insight offered by passionate love is that its course never did run true because the recognition of the loved object's difference lies close to the wisdom of love. One does not love the image of the lover—the lover's beauty or any representation of it—but the "face," whose gestures command our passionate and moral attention but also resist being fixed as an essence. What is loved in the lover defies representation for just this reason, Finkielkraut argues, showing us that the idea of representation and the actuality of love, which loves precisely what cannot be fixed, are at odds: "Passion silences everything adjectival." Modern skepticism, on the other hand, seeks to disenchant the frustrations of love, discovering desire once more in the lover's persistence and masochism as the secret telos of every lover on a fruitless quest.

The Wisdom of Love reclaims that skepticism for modernity, without sacrificing its religious sources. Finkielkraut's work makes a case for a love that belies any fusional model of passion, and heaves closer to the Jewish tradition in which only respect for Others—not absorption or negation of them when they reject our embrace—can redeem the world for all. The Jewish position in multiculturalism, for Finkielkraut, is a position that belongs to the Enlightenment tradition that seeks "equal rights" but demands a recognition of and respect for difference, admiring a passion that seeks to attain its social, or personal, object while refusing to cancel the Otherness of passion's call. This "Jewish" position in multiculturalism is thus also a universalist one. Like Walter Benjamin's belief in an Ursprache or original language, it grounds the right to difference in the original unity that allows us to understand one another. Such a unity sees the encounter with the "foreign" as the messianic hope that such unity might one day be regained, while difference is preserved.[18]

THE ETHICS OF RECOGNITION: THE FACE

The Wisdom of Love therefore rejects the alternatives in the multicultural debate that have been defined by the cultural right. As Charles Taylor reminds us, there "must be something midway between the inauthentic and homogenizing demand for recognition and equal worth, on the one hand, and the self-immurement in ethnocentric standards, on the other."[19] For Finkielkraut, the image of that position between homogenized equality and nostalgic ethnic unity is what Lévinas calls "the ethical relation, the face to face."[20] What Lévinas analyzes as the face-to-face encounter between self and Other stands behind the critical project that is *The Wisdom of Love*. Marked with an ineradicable specificity that totalitarian rage seeks to cancel, the face of the Other is for Finkielkraut also the universal call to justice that cannot be evaded, and a particularity that serves as a source of national and individual passions. The encounter between these alternatives, and the choices they have asked us to make in the twentieth century, are the subject of this work. This is a book that reminds us in many different ways that the impossible demand to recognize difference in our own terms and passions, without canceling it, is both the wisdom of love and the ethical demand itself.

Acknowledgments

We would like to thank Jennifer Kelley for her expert bibliographic help with this translation, and Colby College for making the Hume Center available as a research site. We are also grateful to Jon Klancher, Willi Goetschel, Stephan Dowden, and Doris Sommer for helpful, critical readings of the introduction. Finally, we would like to express our appreciation to Karen and Dorota for their continued support.

Preface

In many languages there is a word that signifies both charity and greed, generosity and avarice, the act of giving and of taking: that word is *love*. In this single expression, a being's ardent desire for all that would fulfill it merges with absolute self-denial and becomes one. Both the heights of self-interest and our deepest concern for the Other bring us to speak of love.

But who believes in selflessness these days? Who still accepts benevolent behavior as legal tender? Since the dawn of modern times, every genealogy of morality traces altruism's roots back to greed and demystifies the origins of noble action as acquisitive desire. Any shedding of the self will reveal some debt to the self; there is no beneficence without compensation, no generosity without its underlying, symbolic gratifications, no offering, finally, that does not betray the imperialistic need to act upon and possess the Other. Giving is always predatory, our acts always lucrative. Such thoughts immediately spring to mind; always on the lookout, we seek only to unmask the ever-present reality of egocentrism lurking behind devotion's facade. As humans, we are stripped of the capacity to give. Relieved of religious or moral scruples and committed to the facts alone, positivist thinking retains no trace of love beyond the need to appropriate; only normative thinking values disinterestedness over universal voracity, the law of every man for himself: love of his fellow man defines man as he should be, or as he one day will be, when History has cleaned the slate of his oppressive past.

While our need for insight has opened this divide, it is by

Preface

no means certain that relegating love of our fellow man to an ideal sphere gives us better purchase on the real. On the contrary: perhaps we truly need archaic concepts and a different storyline to understand our fundamental relationship to others, a narrative that grasps the bond of love as fully as it does the hatred of the other man.

The Wisdom of Love

I

The Encounter with the Other

Shortly after the Liberation, Jean Wahl founded the Collège Philosophique in Paris on the Rue de la Montagne-Sainte-Geneviève. Now forgotten, this institution was for several years the vital center of French intellectual life. It was there that lectures for the general public, new research, and daring new avenues of thought could be sampled—ideas that did not fit the mold of the universities or the major journals, ever more absorbed in fighting the major intellectual battles of the day.

The Collège Philosophique is best described as an island preserved from every sort of conformity, an enclave at once removed from a nascent political tyranny and liberated from the cowardice of a sleepy philosophical tradition. Intellectual experimentation could be pursued without compromise, without inhibitions, and at times recklessly, answering only to itself.

The general climate of the institute was marked by universal openness and a curiosity that knew no bounds. No topic, nothing, however trivial or subaltern it might appear, fell outside philosophy's field of investigation. There were no more privileged or isolated areas of thought; a priori philosophical truths were put aside: the search for meaning was followed wherever it led. Fundamental information was not immediately winnowed from the insignificant: traditional distinctions were called into question. Suspending its former criteria, philosophy *compromised* itself, debased itself, visited areas of existence it had never before acknowledged:

thought was allowed to wander in quotidian domains previously regarded as unworthy of its curiosity. The philosopher felt liberated: he was no longer that serious man, imprisoned by a rigid conception of what is and is not important, condemned to a life sentence of the great questions. He was reconciled with daily life, and all subjects drew his attention, especially those he had not previously been able to investigate without tumbling from his pedestal.

How can we explain this sudden bulimia? By the almost simultaneous discovery of Hegel, Husserl, and Heidegger. After them, there was no way philosophy could blithely respond to the question "What am I?" with the Cartesian response "I am a thinking being."[1] Human reality could no longer be defined exclusively as reason or understanding, but by two fundamental plots: the encounter with the other and the relation to being. Plots, and not knowledge, for knowledge offers no special access to being or to others. Such access is offered, on the contrary, by phenomena that precede reflection, impalpable discomforts, states of being long held to be blind or merely derivative, symptoms of something else. Immense upheaval: the split between "subjective" and "objective"—between the world as we perceive it, and what is only a manifestation of ourselves—became hazy. Ultimate questions were now rooted in run-of-the-mill experience, and facts believed to be of purely psychic significance displayed their revelatory power. Anxiety, for instance, was no longer a character trait or a momentary lapse into the irrational, but a direct and irreducible route to nothingness.

While Freudianism extended the psychological method to all of human experience, phenomenology (since that is the name of this method) revealed, in contrary fashion, the metaphysical drama played out in the banalities of life. Plebeian concerns thus opened up to reveal aristocratic problems of thought. As Lévinas put it in his introduction to *Time and the Other,* a collection of lectures delivered at the Collège Philosophique, "The words designating what people were always concerned with, without daring to imagine it in a speculative discourse, took the rank of categories."[2]

At the time, the work of Emmanuel Lévinas was known and appreciated by only a group of specialists: his words were heard at the Collège Philosophique but found little echo in the great postwar debates. It would take more than thirty years for this subtle and demanding philosopher to find an audience beyond philosophy's technicians, and for his work to finally resonate in intellectual life. The intellectual world, whether sure of the course history would take or immersed in revolutionary urgency—when it was not ignoring the existence of Lévinas's thought entirely—had long considered such meditations as *outmoded,* lacking *contemporary* significance or concern for our fellow men. Marxism's decline has eliminated this obstacle: today Lévinas is being discovered and appreciated not only for the gravity of his ethical concern but even more for the unexpected charm with which his novelistic themes have enlivened the austere discourse of philosophy.

What is existence? Lévinas responds to this majestic question with an inconsequential drama, the very drama whose affliction Oblomov must bear. Oblomov, that famous character of Russian literature, suffers from a common malady—laziness—that he carries to the radical extreme of wholesale revulsion toward any kind of activity whatsoever. He aspires to absolute tranquility, and he can never quite reach his ideal. Even his slothful life as a landlord, living off the income of his lands, is far too consuming. He has to supervise the management of his domain, visit his tenants—in a word, live. But his monumental laziness militates against any such concessions. So he shuts himself in, flees from animation into

3

apathy, even refuses to allow the light of day to penetrate the four walls of his room. No such luck! There is always too much going on for Oblomov, too much commotion and hubbub in his inaction. Even if he were to stop opening his mail, delegate the work of administering his property to others, chase off the last seekers of favor, spend his life in bed, break every connection with the outside world once and for all in order to slip into absolute indolence, undisturbed torpor—this work, this weight, this duty, this inescapable undertaking would still remain Oblomov's: existence. There is no such thing as going on strike against being. Oblomov hurdles these obstacles to his repose only to hurl himself against this insurmountable stumbling block. His lazy sighs are to no avail.

To exist, as Lévinas tells us in his lectures at the Collège Philosophique, is a burden and not a gift. The self is bound to itself, constantly encumbered with and mired in itself. Existence imposes its terms with all the force of a contract etched in stone. One is not: one is oneself. The phrase echoes Sartre's formulation in *The Age of Reason:* "to exist is just that, to imbibe oneself without being thirsty."

Such is the obligation that inspires Oblomov's "impotent and joyless aversion."[3] His laziness stands as an a priori protest against the burden of existence. Behind the "I must do this" overwhelming him each morning with its tiresome demands, Oblomov discovers an "I must be" that is all the more inexorable and discouraging. For this slothful figure is not the possessor of a tragic flaw, nor the victim of a past trauma, nor the representative of a class beset by impotence, but a being who unsuccessfully refuses the condition of being. More than a symbol of society or sign of neurosis, his lethargy is an ontological state. In flight from every kind of intrigue, unsuited for grand tragedies, Oblomov bears witness to this fundamental tragedy: in fatigue or atony, we recoil in the face of existence, dragging our feet, wishing we could call time-out, but escape is impossible: man is stuck with being.

FEAR IN THE DARK

In order to grasp this problem, two contradictory hindrances must be overcome: a sarcasm mixed with fear and the self-assurance that results from an inferiority complex. Philosophy provokes such an ambivalent response in the educated reader—once known as the honest man—and scares him away. A skeptic, he has only a limited confidence in those nebulous philosophic constructions that allow no vestige of external reality within their bounds, in those systems that disembody life at the very moment their proffered explanation claims to lay it bare. It bothers him to see human experience set off in abstruse texts, transformed, in an act of high impudence, into an esoteric domain to be worked on solely by a select group of specialists. The layperson cannot forgive philosophers for appropriating everyone's problems, for professionalizing them, obscuring them, and finally handing them back in a language that excludes the general public.

But this mocking reader is also an intimidated reader: rejecting speculative abstraction in favor of common sense, he at the same time feels too limited, too stubbornly down-to-earth to be permitted entrance to these discussions of the initiated. Resigning himself to the sorrowful fact that thought has its princes, that he is not gifted with the knack for pure thought, he gives up, sensing his inadequacy. If he avoids or skirts philosophy, he does so piously, in a melancholy spirit of deference and resignation: he is convinced the task is above him. Generally speaking, he is less frightened by liberal education as a whole than he is by this peremptory and sovereign discipline that confronts the essential without mediation. Today's prevailing impression of the philosophical pursuit sees it as both regal and ridiculous: philosophy appears before us as the premier field of intellectual inquiry and as illusion at its worst, as both the grammar of thought and as absolute verbal vanity. Ill will (isn't this really nit-picking?) and humility (who am I to ascend that summit?) unite to divide philosophy from living, breathing culture. Phenomenology, we know, has failed to heal this breach. True, phenomenology has shown that we comprehend the world not by knowledge but through our concerns, through adventures and even frivolous undertakings, and that "things small" offer access to the "great." All this demonstrates a marked preference for minutiae, but to no avail: it is a lost cause, and these arguments remain powerless. If the word *being* appears in the middle of a text, most readers drop it immediately, moved by a mixture of disdain and terror.

Lévinas is indebted, however, to that grand Heideggerian distinction between being and existence—between that which exists (individual, species, collectivity) and the act or event of existence—for his success in bringing the most childish and least speculative experience of all back to life: the fear a child experiences when alone at night. Lévinas brings it back to life; he does not interpret it psychologically. The "new philosophical shudder,"[4] introduced by the author of *Being and Time,* made it possible to go beyond the mother's explanation of this scene: when the child cannot sleep and all lights are out, he starts listening to the night's impalpable whisper. What he apprehends, in all its purity, is existence without any existing entity: being's anonymous form.

All is silence in the room; things seem to return to the void; and yet, the nimble ear hears a strange clamor in the stillness. Nothing is there, but the emptiness is thick, like tranquility in an uproar, its nothingness inhabited by scattered rustling sounds and inexplicable explosions: nothing is there except being in general, the inevitable murmur of *there is*. *There is,* always, even when there is not anything: this is what the child discovers. What emerges is a fear, not of the monstrous shapes or fantastic images that appear under cover of darkness, but the fear of being absorbed by this shapeless existence. Childish fright unmasks existence amidst its completely impersonal, continuous aspect. It never stops. What never stops? The event of being.

What is fearful in the silence of night is not death but being. We are less terrified by existence coming to an end than by this *incessant* existence enveloping us. There is no intermission in this concert, not the slightest break in the seamless continuity of being. Thus while the child in the dark undergoes a Heideggerian experience, he simultaneously sets himself apart from such philosophical terms. In his anguish, no revelation of the void takes place: fearful, he discovers only its impossibility. At the heart of utter silence, when daily activities are set aside and everything sleeps around him, an almost inaudible lapping sound rises up in place of the void, as an atmosphere and a material sensation. Existence has not been abolished. A silly fear? What is important in this feeling results, perhaps, from an experience more decisive than our anxiety before the void: the horror of being.

At dawn, each thing rediscovers its allotted space; every object reclaims its name. Being veils itself, scattering into different realities. Even the self returns to its identity. It rises, emerging from indeterminacy, and assumes, side by side with others, a being that is once again its own. Light personifies the world once more, dispelling the nightmare of the *there is*. But the victory is incomplete: to exist means to suspend being's anonymity, to fashion one's own domain within existence, a universe of one's own—which we call identity—but at the same time to be unable to flee or to avoid existence. Existence means that one remains, by virtue of selfhood's bonds, stuck in the snare of being. Sartre says—and here he is very close to Lévinas—that existence is a burden that man cannot set aside. This weight, this impossibility of escape, this continual presence of the self to the self is the tribute every one of us pays the universality of the *there is*. And this, as we have seen, is the origin of Oblomov's lassitude. For beyond their circumstantial causes, laziness and weariness are metaphysical pouts, moments when the existent begins to dislike the existence in which he feels permanently trapped. He realizes that the pose he assumes is not salvation but a new encumbrance:

The I always has one foot caught in its own existence. Outside in face of everything, it is inside of itself, tied to itself. It is forever bound to the existence which it has taken up. This impossibility for the ego to not be a self constitutes the underlying tragic element in the ego, the fact that it is riveted to its own being.[5]

A tragedy of captivity within being, not of anxiety in the face of the void. A tragedy of the bond of the self to itself, not of the power that foreign force exerts upon it. Our intuitive philosophy sees liberty (the possession of self) as the opposite of alienation (superiority or domination by the other). By intuitive philosophy I mean the most common-sense morality (being one's own master) as well as modern conceptions of liberation: both claim a permanent autonomy for the subject and seek to assure a full field for its realization and to emancipate the individual from those external forces in whose thrall he remains. But lassitude, weariness, or insomnia—conditions too often neglected—find little comfort in this tradition, in this modernity: such feelings discover the deepest kind of alienation in the boredom of being oneself. It is not the *other* that imposes original servitude, but *being:* our first master is the self that encumbers and unceasingly doubles the ego. The initial constraint by which consciousness discovers itself bound is the bond of identity itself. Deeper and more determining, perhaps, than the need to be one's self, to find oneself, to purge the self of the taint of the foreign, is the dream of separation from the self, of escaping identity's fated return.

THE FACE

In 1947, Lévinas published *Existence and Existents,* with a book jacket that read: "Here anxiety is not the question." In an equally provocative fashion, the crucial question raised by this book's grand analyses of social relations, of our encounter with other men, does not turn on the notion of struggle. Provocative indeed, for along with Heidegger's concept of anxiety, Hegel's Master-Slave dialectic—the war of consciousnesses—dominated the intellectual life of the time. To illustrate the foundational nature of such struggle, Sartre chooses the most peaceful and insignificant situation for his example:

I am in a public park. Not far away there is a lawn and along the edge of that lawn there are benches. A man passes by those benches.[6]

The setting is neutral, suspense nonexistent. It is a scene of absolute calm, with nothing going on. No relationship connects me with this unknown man walking in the same garden as I. What strikes me, what remains unavoidable, is the very fact of others. And this fact is a violent one. With a single glance, the gentle stroller banishes me from paradise, announces my downfall. I am seen, and that is all it takes to change my world. I was pure freedom, a consciousness out-

side any particular image, "a transparency without memory
or consequence"; then, I find that I have suddenly become
someone in particular. Observed, examined, measured, or
even just perceived by a foreign gaze, I possess a nature I
cannot challenge, one that does not belong to me. My being
is externalized, wrapped up in the being of another. In other
words, this entry of others into my surroundings produces
a double malaise: his gaze reduces me to the status of an
object, an object over which I have no control since it is "for
another." I am mired and dispossessed, fallen and alienated:
the simple fact of being seen leaves me frozen, trapped in
and robbed of myself. Under the gaze of the other I become
this or that, with no hold over this petrified reality.

*the Other is for me simultaneously the one who has stolen my
being from me and the one who causes "there to be" a being which
is my being.*[7]

And so, just by looking at me, the other gains the upper
hand. Sartre described all forms of desire—from sadistic violence to the sweetness of sentimental love—as so many
tricks, so many ruses of war the subject deploys to free himself from this snare. Confronted by others who possess me
because they see me as I will never see myself, I become "the
project of recovering my being."[8]

The relation with the other, not reflection, is the foun-
dation of self-consciousness. Human experience is social before it is rational. Social and bellicose. Life is a novel in
which all turns on conflict: this is Hegel's troublesome truth.
Everything is combat, even the sweetest moments, when
those idyllic gestures seem a celebration of peace, even the
caressing melody of transparent souls, even the melting of
two bodies into one. Phenomenological description uses
merciless severity to expose the tapestry of aggression and
machinations behind the innocence of the caress. "The caress

is not simple stroking; it is a shaping. In caressing the Other, I bring about the birth of her flesh, under my fingers. The caress is the ensemble of those rituals which incarnate the Other."[9] The exquisite meeting of skin? Actually, it is a clever way of ambushing the other, who, by renouncing his gaze and his freedom, becomes a docile presence. The caress is an incitement to passivity, an attempt to force the desired state of being back into the other's flesh, so that there is no escape, so that I no longer have to live under the other's gaze. However tender or fervent it may be, the caress is motivated by a desire to render the Other innocuous, disarmed, objectified, enclosed, to keep the Other from being able to transcend me in every way, through sheer presence of being. An insidious way for me to take revenge, to end my exposure, dependence, and possession, and, instead, to finally be the boss. Through the caress, I freeze and enervate the one whose gaze entrapped me in my being. There are certainly no truces when the battle of consciousnesses is joined. The soldier on leave remains a combatant: his rest and relaxation a ruse of war.

What interests Lévinas, like Sartre, is the classic situation where we are not alone. And faithful to Hegel's example, he locates the subject's origin in the intrigue tying him to the other. Yet his version of this plot is unique, neither an unfolding conflict nor, for that matter, an idyllic scene. To describe the encounter with the Other, Lévinas challenges the pastoral and conflictual models alike. In short order, he dispatches both the foolishness of unambiguous reciprocity and the pitiless image of the struggle for recognition. Without surrendering in any way to the schmaltzy lures of bygone utopias, without falling for an affected nostalgia that optimistically awaits the return of brotherhood's golden age, Lévinas refuses to grant to war the privileged status of an original state. At a time when hardheaded insight in both philosophy and politics seems to have been confused with the notion of conflict, here is a philosopher who dares to affirm: "It is by no means certain that, at the beginning, there was war."[10] War is not the original situation of the encounter; nor is peace, we should add, if peace is defined as hearts joined in spontaneous sympathy, "the happy encounter of brotherly souls, who greet one another and converse."[11] The social relationship is "the miracle of moving out of oneself,"[12] which only afterward begins its alternation between the poles of harmony and war. Before becoming the power that menaces, attacks, or bewitches the self, the other is the crucial force that shatters the bond of self-identity, that relieves, diverts—that liberates the self from itself and thus delivers the existent from the weight of its own existence. Before it is gaze, the other is face.

A face, not a sketch, a fleshed-out figure evoking disgust or admiration. A face, not a text in which the soul's movements are inscribed and held out for eventual interpretation. "A work of art," writes Valéry, "should always teach us that we haven't previously seen what we are seeing." Lévinas's body of philosophic work teaches us not to see the face better or to see it in a new way but to cease identifying the face with the claims of vision. His work does not awaken our drowsy perceptions, casting new light on a reality that we grasp in merely utilitarian or mechanical terms, but instead awakens us from perception itself. Regardless of whether such perception is aesthetic or disciplinary, whether it appreciates the face as a play of appearances or as a richness of signs. Whether it seeks a sign or has grace bestowed upon it. Whether perceptual passion is stirred by the countenance or its secret. Vision surely inhabits the face, but this optical kinship should not lead one astray: the face is the single prey that the image-hungry hunter can never catch. The eye always returns empty-handed from the face of the Other, who slips out of the forms he assumes, plays representation for the fool, and constantly opposes the gaze in which I fix him.

The way in which the other presents himself, exceeding the idea of the other in me, we here name face. This mode does not consist in figuring as a theme under my gaze, in spreading itself forth as a set of qualities forming an image. The face of the Other at each moment destroys and overflows the plastic image it leaves me, the idea existing to my own measure . . . the adequate idea.[13]

The face, or the narrow escape. Its determining characteristic is resistance to definition, the way it never allows itself to be cornered by my most pointed questions or even by my most penetrating gaze. The Other always is more than what I know of him, always escapes my grasp. This surplus, this constant excess of the being that takes aim at the intention that would fix him, goes by the name *face*. "To encounter a man is to be kept on alert by an enigma."[14]

The face is thus not the physical form we normally understand to be designated by this word but the resistance of our fellow man to his own appearance, the way in which he absolves himself of his image, makes his presence felt as something more than his shape alone, leaves nothing in my hands but his skin, when I thought I had captured his truth.

This elusiveness and defeat are both beneficial. To move beyond the self means a sacrifice of power because the Other refuses assimilation and does not become mine, because my experiences do not represent inevitable steps toward a fated homecoming. The only thing in the world capable of truly separating me from myself, the only thing that sends me on adventures other than my own Odyssey, is the face of the other. I approach the face; I do not absorb it: a wondrous weakness, without which even the most extravagant life would be as monotonous as a voyage from the self to the self.

Put on a good face. Do an about face. Save face. Keep a straight face: such expressions highlight the two opposed meanings the word *face* carries in everyday speech. Face designates both appearance—an essence hidden and given away there, the dissimulating tricks that prevent our gaze from reaching a being's truth—and that truth itself, when the masks are finally torn away. Between confession and performance, between facade and avowal, what is peculiarly fascinating about the face is the way it simultaneously offers and masks itself as an object of knowledge, making it the singular bodily site that both reveals and conceals the soul. We make a face and involuntarily give a clue to our most secret emotions. We put on makeup to please or to mislead watchful eyes, presenting our face to the world like "an invisible secret" (Sartre). We all hope to tame our faces, to use them as a weapon, to hypnotize, or to construct an unbreachable front; we all try to hide our dirty deeds behind a deceptive smile or our disappointments behind a jaunty air. The most adept succeed; the rascal souls of the less gifted reveal to the world the personal trauma they strove to conceal.

But, as Lévinas tells us, this opposition between Being and appearance is not the final word. The face's nakedness exists prior to this dualism of exposure and concealment in that vertiginous boundary zone where body and soul meet. The face of the Other is naked before it is artificial or authentic, interesting or banal, seductive or repulsive; before it is either confessional, as if divulging its ultimate secret, or opaque, like an indecipherable hieroglyph: the face is naked, bereft of its most intimate or salient features, beyond lies as well as truth, separated from its reflection in me, withdrawn, as if lacking self-presence. "The face is the reality par excellence in which a being is not presented by its qualities."[15]

But this reality outside my grasp is also an unprotected

surface: a nakedness that resists everything attributed to it and that no garment can clothe. The body's most inaccessible part, the face, is also its most vulnerable. Both transcendent and destitute, the face is so lofty that it escapes me, while shedding its own malleable essence, and so weak that its weakness inhibits me when I gaze into its helpless eyes. Distinct, it exceeds my power. Unprotected, defenseless, it lays itself bare, making me ashamed of my cold composure. The face resists me and calls upon me: I am not a neutral observer but am obligated by the face. Responsibility toward the Other precedes thought. The initial face-to-face encounter is ethical; the aesthetic is a secondary effect.

The face calls out to me for help: at my mercy, exposed, infinitely fragile, and piercing as a broken cry. There is something imperious in its plea. I do not feel sorry for such misery because the face's demand that I come to its rescue is an act of violence. The face's humble nakedness not only claims my solicitude as its due but also—as one might say, if the word were not subject to immediate derision—demands my charity. For my presence alone does not suffice when the Other turns his face toward me: he demands that I be there *for him* and not just *with him*.

Thus I am not the one who determines whether I will be egotistical or selfless: it is the face that, in its nakedness, takes me beyond self-interest. The Good comes to me from without, the ethical falls from above, and it is in spite of myself that my "own being turns into being for another."[16]

Love is not at our beck and call: that is superficial wisdom. The face of the Other makes me love's intimate or at least makes indifference impossible. Of course, I can always look the other way; I can disobey or revolt against love's demands, but it is never within my power to cease listening. To set the rigor of the law against the fervor of love is therefore a futile affair. The face harries me, demands that I place society before the self, subordinates me to its weakness: in short, it *legislates that I love it.* The face is superior to me, because it refuses to let itself be identified, and is inferior to me, because it remains at my mercy. But humility and haughtiness are the two sides of the supremacy it sustains, of the domination it holds over my being.

The face imposes itself on me without my being able to remain deaf to its appeal, nor to forget — in fact, without my being able to cease being responsible for its misery. [17]

WRINKLED SKIN

*To age is gradually to retire from
the world of appearances.* Goethe

The face is not a landscape. To scrutinize it, no matter how patiently and insightfully you take up the task, is already to have missed it, to have confused the face with its effigy. "The face with which the Other turns to me is not reabsorbed in a representation of the face."[18] One exception exists, nevertheless, to this resolutely nonfigurative approach. Lévinas, for once, sets aside his proclivity for abstraction.

The other man commands through his face which is not enclosed in the form of what appears, naked, stripped of his shape, of his very presence that might still disguise him as his own portrait; wrinkled skin, the trace of itself, a presence which, at each moment, is a retreat into the hollow of death with the possibility of no return. [19]

Wrinkled skin: it is the only distinguishing feature, the only observable mark that the philosopher of the face allows the reader. But far from embodying the Other, this singular material feature only underscores once more the Other's evanescence. Though concrete and visible, such wrinkles spirit the face away from my visual powers. By its weathering and by the furrows gouged upon it, the face both evades me and commands me not to leave it alone. Precariously present, as if eaten away by an absence, my neighbor does not fully consist of what I see: wrinkles let him evade the capturing gaze, carry him away, and absolve him of contact with my life. And in this escape, the countenance asserts its force. Wrinkled skin beckons me and carts me off, summons and abandons me, eludes me and endangers me in a way that would not even encumber me if the face were not, in its very presence, about to disappear.

As everyone knows, "there are only young faces." For what is old age, after all, but inevitable deterioration, the loss of distinctive traits, the ravages time wreaks upon beings, leaving them unrecognizable in the end? Age, for us, means the devastation of the face. Lévinas takes the opposite point of view. Whatever its chronological age, he implies, *the face is always old,* not disfigured but defined by age. An imperceptible hint of failure dims the fullness or grace of the most youthful profiles. The wrinkles that spoil the beauty of the face at the same time grant it that evasive and necessary reality that becomes my responsibility. Wrinkled skin: the Other is not the adversary of the self but rather the obligation conferred upon it.

SHAME

The Talmud contains the following passage: A sage says to his son, "What a poorly written document." The son replies, "I didn't write that, it was Judah the tailor." The father responds, "Don't slander him!" Another time, while reading a chapter from the Psalms, the same sage exclaims, "What a model of good writing!" "I didn't write it, it was Judah the tailor," said the son. "Don't slander him!" the father again cuts him off. And it is explained: one should never say good things about others, for that is how we end up speaking ill of them.

A cursory reading of this story teaches the moral that all praise carries within itself the seeds of its opposite. Man being what he is, with envy reigning supreme over the complex of human passions, we exalt the merits of another even while we delight at the thought of those treacheries that will soon cut him down to size. The more the other distinguishes himself, the more I resent him for the admiration his exploits force me to feel: he will have to pay up later for the adulation I have heaped upon his successes and talents. My words of praise call out for vengeance. And so prudence demands that we suppress praise so as not to succumb later to the temptation to malign.

This lesson in disillusionment, however, hardly exhausts the wealth of meaning in the Talmudic tale. The sage responds twice to his son in exactly the same terms, marking an equivalent as well as a causal relation between apology and slander. Whether we bow before his craft or ridicule his clumsiness, Judah the tailor always reassumes his status as descriptively *qualified*. That is the fundamental violence of the scene, not the name-calling or flattering terms that are deployed. To respond to the most offhanded compliment with a decisive "Do not slander" is to denounce the aggressiveness of this innocent gesture: to speak of a being is to inflict upon him the treatment as a third person singular.

If we were to follow the Talmudic injunction to the letter, we would no doubt be reduced to silence or to a language of pure invocation: to say "he" would effectively mean speaking ill of someone. But this moral is not meant to be applied rigidly: it simply reminds us that the Other can never be just another topic, and that "he," pronoun of the nonperson, is truly "the nastiest word in the language."[20] We talk about our neighbor for all sorts of good reasons but also to avoid responding to him. We heap predicates over the nakedness of his face to avoid hearing his call. We categorize him rather than respond to his summons: such is the essence of calumny, and lies are nothing but an intensified version of this fundamental evasion.

Our sage, we can be sure, would chalk up today's generous slogans celebrating difference—the new value placed on ways of life or ethnic traits that were once spurned and disdained—as so much more calumny. True, there is nothing worse than elevating one's own mode of being into the universal norm and thereby denying the humanity of those whose customs are foreign to us or who sport a different skin color. And cultural diversity must be ceaselessly defended against ethnocentric arrogance. This valorization of difference, however, and the rejection of difference share a common thread: *the assigning of difference,* the process of confusing one's neighbor with his attributes. Considerable progress has been made in moving from the scorn or fear of blacks to the formula "Black is beautiful"; but in both cases, the countenance remains chained to its manifestations, sentenced to the uninterrupted expression of an unequivocal message. Idolatry perpetuates slander.

If the Other is what he is, he ceases to be other. His exteriority is annexed, and his commanding power is dissolved to benefit his image. The Other is not set free by granting him a unique, even prestigious essence: this frees you, not him. In short, a face that is defined by its difference is a face stripped of its otherness. It no longer accuses; it no longer implores: it ceases to shame us. Through calumny, order has been restored.

Our difficulties before the Other, in effect, go deeper than our notions of him. Whether true or false, full of praise or malignity, such notions probably originate in the selfsame desire: to escape the fundamental fact of moral challenge. "Out of shame, we confer on the Other an unquestionable presence," Sartre writes. And Lévinas could certainly lay claim to such a formulation, which defines our primary social experience as one of malaise. Yet the other, conceived of by Sartre as the gaze that freezes me into objectivity, locking my nimble liberty up within being, is described by Lévinas in terms of the face, the countenance of the Other that contests my tranquil self-assured right to Being. What brings me to a halt, petrifying my spontaneity, is not the objectifying gaze of the Other but his isolation, naked and defenseless. What suddenly makes me flush, what embarrasses me, is not the alienation of my liberty but my liberty itself: it is not that I feel attacked but that I am the attacker. My neighbor's face accuses me of egotistically holding on to Being, of tossing aside any consideration for all that is not me. The timidity that results is the moral uneasiness welling up in me. This shame brings us neither to open conflict nor to the death struggle of two consciousnesses but to scruples: the awareness of my natural injustice.

In this way, the face of the Other proves doubly beneficial: it frees the self from self-concern and deflates its smugness and arrogance. Lévinas gives the simple words "I am" either the tragic meaning of imprisonment or the triumphant sense of a vital force. Boredom and imperialism. Fatality and savage vitality. "The enchainment to itself, where the ego suffocates in itself,"[21] the self holding fast to Being, a condition in which the ego — comprehending the foolishness of its desire or its preference for the wisdom of self-interest — still remains concerned with itself alone. Being, that original experience of alienation, is both a condition in which one is riveted to oneself and a state of original violence in which one charges into the world without hesitation. Being means being swallowed up and at the same time diffused into the world, forming an unhappy but inseparable couple *with* the self, but also a being that remains *for* itself, sovereignly indifferent to all else. This double mode of Being gives a novelesque flavor and ethical content to the face and the tangled web it weaves. By shaming the subject's devastating dynamism and self-interested motives, the face commands: it attains the power of an imperative. By turning the self from itself, the face soothes and seduces: with its adventurous attraction, the face is "a fine risk to be run."[22]

THE BEAST IN THE JUNGLE

Lévinas's originality consists not so much in his emphasis on morality, in the midst of a political century, as in his *transposition* of morality into a new schema. He locates Good not at the end, in the Utopian horizon, the glorious future of historical fulfillment, but at the beginning, in the age-old experience of the encounter with Others. Not struggle but ethics becomes the fundamental meaning of Being for others. The face-to-face encounter with the other man evokes responsibility rather than conflict. The face calls to me as if I were involved with it in a way that precedes any self-confrontation. "The ethical relation is anterior to the opposition of freedoms, the war which, in Hegel's view, inaugurates History."[23] This does not mean that peace reigned before war, but that *ethical violence* precedes the contest between consciousnesses and the adversarial relation. The Good seizes me, holding on without my consent. It chooses me before I have chosen it: I can disobey, but I cannot escape it. Evil is incapable of eradicating shame, of breaking with or repudiating subjection to the face of the Other. "Evil manifests its sinfulness, that is to say responsibility in spite of its own refusal of responsibilities. Neither next to, nor facing Good, but in second place, underneath, lower than Good."[24]

What is loving your neighbor? One aspect of subjectivity, a modality of the human condition. Not a program but a drama; not a quality but a matter of fate. Under the influence of the face, goodness approaches the subject like deliverance or destiny. Morality does not spring from the active "I want to," where the virtuous outlook is traditionally rooted: distinct from any exercise of will, morality anchors itself in a passivity we are not accustomed to regarding as ethical ground. In spite of myself, self-interest turns into love, and the Other becomes my concern. Ethical concern: an involuntary wandering, the rout of a self-concern that is lived as boredom or egotistically practiced.

"The most sublime act is to place the Other before the self." Lévinas adds a crucial qualification to Blake's admirable aphorism: such an act results not from any magnanimous resolve but from a summons that cannot be escaped. The sublime makes itself felt amidst the distraction of the will, not in its apotheosis. In order to speak of Good, Lévinas reintroduces outmoded terms such as *disinterest, saintliness,* or *glory,* but gives them an absolutely unexpected location. The language is Corneille's, the plot from Racine. And the same holds true for *agape* and for *eros,* for the love of one's neighbor and romantic love: "No one is not good voluntarily."[25] It is not out of choice that we lose our heads, let our minds stray, cast prudence to the winds, reject the advantageous counsel and forethought of utilitarian reason. We do not decide to act against *our own* interest. Stripped of our own initiative, our consciousness is bound "fatally and as if against our will, for an other who attracts us all the more because he seems to be outside the possibility of meeting because he is so beyond the scope of things that interest us."[26]

In one of his finest short tales, Henry James tells the story of the life, or rather the nonlife, of John Marcher, a man haunted by the strange feeling of having been chosen to live out an extraordinary something, a something he knows nothing about except that it will appear without notice, turning his world upside down: "Something or other lay in wait for him, amid the twists and the turns of the months and the years, like a crouching beast in the jungle."[27]

This something, John Marcher hopes, at the risk of being crushed, will change his completely inactive life into one of true excitement. He prepares himself for the great battle. He places himself in mortal danger. He seeks out the unexpected, knowing only that this spectacle will resemble an animal leaping on its prey. He thus devotes all his attention to catching sight of the shadow this beast casts on the drab web he weaves of his days.

A woman, Mary Bertram, shares this extraordinary secret and agrees to watch for it with John Marcher. An exhausting and fruitless lookout: his monotonous existence is made still worse by the petrified vigilance he takes as his task. Since nothing lives up to expectations, "the years go by and the stroke doesn't fall."[28] The long wait consumes the intimate life of the chosen one and his confidante, until the death of Mary Bertram. Visiting her tomb one day to collect his thoughts, John Marcher comes upon a man suffering the pangs of a recent loss. The minor incident has the force of a revelation: he is struck by the idea of being *Too Late:*

The sight that had just met his eyes named to him, as in letters of quick flame, something he had utterly, insanely missed, and what he had missed made these things a train of fire, made them mark themselves in an anguish of inward throbs. He had seen outside of his life, not learned it within, the way a woman was mourned when she had been loved for herself; such was the force of his conviction of the meaning of the stranger's face, which still flared for him like a smoky torch. It had not come to him, the knowledge, on the wings of experience; it had brushed him, jostled him, upset him, with the disrespect of chance, the insolence of an accident. Now that the illumination had begun, however, it blazed to the zenith, and what he presently stood there gazing at was the sounded void of his life.[29]

By preparing himself for the event, John Marcher became the man to whom nothing happened. He missed out on life the way we miss an appointment, because he identified adventure with the contest of battle, and thus avoided running the risks of passionate love. While waiting to strike down the beast, or to be struck down himself, he sidestepped the real confrontation. Standing at the ready for the most terrifying hand-to-hand combat, Marcher remained blind to the passion of the woman he could have loved, instead of incorporating her into his chimerical dream as his sentinel, searching for the fabulous destiny reserved to him alone. What spared Marcher the violence of the encounter was the stereotypic form in which he conceived the struggle. Willing to submit to suffering without a second thought, but expecting it only in a duel of legendary proportions, he was given the most ironic of punishments: the exemption from suffering, the terrifying and mocking misfortune of having lived safe from all torment, of never having suffered for someone else.

There is room—between struggle and idyll, between the violence of adversity and the serenity of affection—for another form of concern, another model of encountering the world: an ethical model, according to Lévinas, and an amorous one in James's short story. All of this points to the conclusion that morality and passion are connected in ways neglected by the moralists of yesterday and by today's militants of desire.

2

The Beloved Face

No love exists as a simple, bodily mechanism, even (or especially)
if it is madly attached to its object, which does not prove our power
to call ourselves into question, offer proof of our capacity for ab-
solute devotion, or testify to our metaphysical meaning. Merleau-
Ponty

THE ARGUMENT

In *Sylvia,* Emmanuel Berl tells the extraordinary tale of his
break with Marcel Proust. The scene took place in 1917, in
the room where the novelist lived in seclusion to write *Re-*
membrance of Things Past. Berl recounts the amazing news
to his friend: he has found Sylvia. After four years of silence,
he wrote to the young woman he had met in a hotel in Evian
and asked her to marry him. Just when he had given up all
hope, he received an answer, in which Sylvia gave him per-
mission to join her. "Truly everything seemed clear. Sylvia
was anything but a frivolous woman. I was engaged."[1]

Berl tries to share his happiness and, at the same time, to
offer himself as living proof that some hearts are meant for
one another. For the longest while, in fact, Proust had used
the time they shared together to "catechize" his interlocutor,
instructing Berl with tireless zeal about man's solitary nature
and the ineluctably disastrous fate to which the passions are
bound. Mercilessly, Proust had shattered every kind of sentimental illusion: "For him it was not just a probable hy-
pothesis that communication between one person and another was impossible; it was an article of faith."[2] But Sylvia's
story seems to escape such pessimism: a mutual recognition

had occurred between two beings, a genuine encounter, and Berl does not want to waste this chance to point it out to Proust, if only by offering a few exceptions to his overly bleak view of affection's course.

The story of this miracle does nothing to lift Proust's spirits: he is alarmed. A few words from a young woman, and his faithless disciple has already cast aside the difficult truth he had sought to instill: reciprocity is not the truth of love but a mirage, a misunderstanding, or a passing affair. Dreams of mutual attachment are a mistake, based on fecklessness. If man would honestly confront his melancholy condition, he would know that feelings do not bridge but deepen the divide that separates two beings. For his part, Berl is stunned to see their blossoming friendship casually sacrificed on the altar of this dogmatic conception of love. He knew Proust was like "an oriental philosopher who lived his doctrine, and indoctrinated his life."[3] But he never believed his friend would break with those close to him whenever their experience or happiness contradicted the wisdom his reflections had attained. The tone between the theorist of inexorable suffering and his detractor becomes ever more shrill; cutting allusions are followed by direct attacks, until finally Proust, crazed with anger, chases off the proselyte of mutual love, hurling insults "like slippers thrown through a bathroom door."[4]

However liberal or open-minded those involved might seek to be, friendship does not easily tolerate differences in opinion. But generally these opinions touch on "serious" subjects, like those that politics provides. Love is seen as too trivial a subject to release such passions. It is not just intransigence that marks the singular tone of the argument between Emmanuel Berl and Marcel Proust but intransigence in a domain usually removed from the feverish contention of ideas. It would be a shame, however, if the scene's comedy concealed what was at stake. In laughable fury, Proust blames the claimant of Sylvia's hand for portraying his malady as a remedy and for betraying the suffering of passion for the illusory union of hearts. Whether Berl's condition is seen as love or as idyll, Proust rejects any such compromise. Far removed from any such disagreement, Lévinas does the same in his most austere philosophical work, *Otherwise Than Being or Beyond Essence:* "in love, where, unless one does not love with love, one has to resign oneself to not being loved."[5]

HESITATION

When Robert de Saint-Loup introduces his mistress to the narrator of *Remembrance of Things Past,* Marcel, to his amazement, recognizes Rachel "When from the Lord . . . she who used to say to the procuress: 'To-morrow evening, then, if you want me for someone, you'll send round for me, won't you?' "[6] The woman whom Saint-Loup prizes before all else, whom he loves at cost to his career and his other affections, who alone can make him suffer or make him happy, and who, within "the same thin and narrow face,"[7] contains all that interests him on earth—this priceless woman began her career in a brothel. This same being, "a mechanical toy" for a bevy of customers, holds "infinitely more importance" in the eyes of her smitten lover "than the Guermantes and all the kings of the earth put together."[8]

This violently contradictory love in the novel prolongs Proust's argument with Emmanuel Berl. Only a kind of iconoclastic rage could have incited Proust to exaggerate Berl's situation beyond the limits of plausibility: he refuses to concede the least objectivity to love or the slightest hope for success. Proust recoils from the deceptive bliss of "You and I"; his phobia toward sentimental babble intensifies to the point of caricature the opposition between the object dreamt of, shaped, composed by the lover and the trivial reality on which it is based. Robert de Saint-Loup transforms a venal woman whom absolutely anyone could have for a louis into an inaccessible figure. Such is the ridiculous power of the human imagination: a tramp who bestowed her favors on a first-come first-serve basis is elevated to the status of an unreachable ideal. The most docile of faces becomes the most overpowering. The lowest creature imaginable is invested with the highest authority, and the professional escort is given the religious nimbus of the transcendent. "Looking at her, Robert and I, we did not both see her from the same side of the mystery."[9]

And so the boundary separating minor obsession from grand passion begins to blur. More like a hero from Molière than from the tradition of mythic lovers, Saint-Loup is "a character following up his one idea, and continually returning to it in spite of incessant interruptions!"[10] He moves us because he is devoted to suffering, but he amuses us as well because a soul who commits the sin of obstinacy and lives in a dream ends by "adjusting things to its own way of thinking, instead of accommodating its thoughts to the things."[11] His love is never entitled to the pleasures of understanding, nor even to the productive tension of true exchange. It is an *idée fixe* or, to borrow the image hazarded by Emmanuel Berl at the argument's overheated height, "hallucinatory masturbation."

In an aside, however, Proust wonders "if it can be said that Rachel the tart was more real than the other."[12] A carefully ventured comment, suddenly casting the scene in a different light, blurring our points of reference, *correcting the satire with hesitation*. If neither of Rachel's contradictory images is accorded the status of definitive truth, then love cannot simply be reduced to the dream of a ridiculous man who searches the external world for a pretext for playing out his fantasies. The narrator, who knows Rachel, and Saint-Loup, who is in love with her, do not see the same side of her mystery. But it is unclear whether one sees clearly and the other is wildly wrong. Truth resides perhaps as much in the passion that feeds on the mystery as in the revelation that destroys it. Love lacks the knowledge of the Other, but knowledge lacks its alterity.

Proust, however, does not try to make up. As is so often the case, the work is less rigid and more subtle than the man, but it does not side with Emmanuel Berl. Whether chimerical or revelatory, passion means suffering in each and every instance: he who loves is not loved in return. Proust never changes this diagnosis. The novel goes back and forth endlessly on how to evaluate love's asymmetry: as a breakdown of communication or as communication of another kind.

There is no question that love is blind. But such dark passion need not necessarily be understood negatively, as a sheer absence of illumination. Perhaps it is necessary not to see but rather to desire and to suffer in order to go beyond qualities such as beauty and to attain that which constitutes the alterity of the Other: his face.

THE ECLIPSE OF BEAUTY

The questioning, anxious, exacting way that we have of looking at the person we love, our eagerness for the word which will give us or take from us the hope of an appointment for the morrow, and, until that word is uttered, our alternate if not simultaneous imaginings of joy and despair, all this makes our attention in the presence of the beloved too tremulous to be able to carry away a very clear impression of her. Perhaps, also, that activity of all the senses at once which yet endeavours to discover with the eyes alone what lies beyond them is overindulgent to the myriad forms, to the different savours, to the movements of the living person whom as a rule, when we are not in love, we immobilise. Whereas the beloved model does not stay still; and our mental photographs of it are always blurred.[13]

The lover is thus a strange creature, capable of forgetting the face that obsesses him. With eyes for a single other, the lover is unable, really, to describe him or her: flagrantly refuting the romantic cliché that exalts love and aesthetic creation as proof of a like sensibility, delicate and tortured. The lover is a mediocre artist, a handcuffed painter, a poet vanquished by the unspeakable. The impassioned and artistic gaze are at loggerheads, not conniving in some illicit alliance. Representation is the privilege (or fate) of those who do not love: the triumph of precision over vagueness, a model substituted for motion.

I no longer really knew how Gilberte's features were composed, save in the heavenly moments when she unfolded them to me: I could remember nothing but her smile. And being unable to visualise that beloved face, despite every effort that I might make to recapture it, I was disgusted to find, etched on my memory with a maddening precision of detail, the meaningless, emphatic faces of the roundabout man and the barley-sugar woman; just as those who have lost a loved one whom they never see again in sleep, are enraged at meeting incessantly in their dreams any number of insupportable people whom it is quite enough to have known in the waking world.[14]

The beloved face is too alive to allow itself to be tamed, even by its own magnificence. Excess attention muddies the loving gaze — excess attention and not, as Berl objects, imagined debauchery. The lover does not project dreamy qualities onto the Other, qualities mined from his own depths; he observes, examines, inspects. Every aspect of the beloved face demands vigilance: furtive sorrows, the faintest grimaces, shadows and shivers, smiles and moods. The beloved face is a tangle of signs he is no longer able to sort out. Art, by contrast, cannot exist without stylization, without the capacity to erase the unessential, so that only the significant remains. Instead, the lover confines himself, against his will, to an unlivable world in which everything is crucially important. A slight tone plunges him into confusion, a brief separation rekindles his anxiety. No details, only hints, and each hint deepens the mystery. "It's nothing serious": his passions prevent any such quip. He has no sense of proportion. The lover, supremely gifted at elevating trifles to the level of tragedy, is a stranger to the respite of insignificance; and this, at the same time, makes the peace offered by the image an impossibility for the beloved face.

A shakily sketched face, but one that brings fear and trembling to the haunted lover. For him, it is a matter of listening more than looking. The Other's words count much more than appearance. The physical attraction of the face comes *after*. After its verdicts: as a presence—promised or refused; as a love—confirmed or conferred to the ambiguity of silence. "The other is assigned to a superior habitat, an Olympus where everything is decided and whence everything descends upon me."[15]

You do not hover over the one you love. The lover lacks both the leisure and the minimal self-possession required to concentrate his visual powers in this way, unable to compensate for the harsh trials of his dispossession with such symbolic appropriation. Thus art is not love's natural form of expression. Love is far more a religion of the face, a faith that forbids the representation of the face. We must not let ourselves be taken by endless celebrations of lyrical passion. The beloved face escapes everything, even the beauty that made love's fruition possible. It is beyond expression:

Physically, she was going through a bad phase; she was putting on weight, and the expressive, sorrowful charm, the surprised, wistful expression of old seemed to have vanished with her first youth. So that she had become most precious to Swann as it were just at the moment when he found her distinctly less good-looking. He would gaze at her searchingly, trying to recapture the charm which he had once seen in her, and no longer finding it. And yet the knowledge that within this new chrysalis it was still Odette who lurked, still the same fleeting, sly, elusive will, was enough to keep Swann seeking as passionately as ever to capture her.[16]

Swann is a connoisseur in every aspect of his life, with a taste for Beauty. But his demanding aesthetic refinement grants one exception: the woman who is not his type, and with whom he falls in love. As a matter of fact, in love, alterity takes over completely, pushing all else to the side—exoticism, looks, social distance, or proximity—and defines the Other's very content. To love is not to demonstrate one's allegiance to Beauty but rather to remove oneself, temporarily, for the length of an obsession, from Beauty's tyrannical criteria. We say only as a kind of approximation, or in deference to tradition, that the beloved's face is beautiful, when in fact the face is transitory, changing, out of reach, fleeting: not an aesthetic presence, but virtual and subject to disappearance. The lover sings of formal perfection, perfection of form, but he is aware, before all else, of its evanescence: that is, that such form is continually contested. Love dethrones Beauty, creating a moment outside its reign, a trembling interval—a paradoxical and sacrilegious moment of disquieting fervor that relegates Beauty to the second tier. The beloved face is neither beautiful nor sublime. It is neither an ineffable splendor nor a masterpiece beyond description but a presence that cannot be enclosed. To put an end to his uncertainty, the lover would no doubt prefer the

Other remain as fixed as an idol, that the movement of its face could become a static Beauty. But such aesthetic idolatry remains, dare we say, a pious wish. The impossibility of halting the ceaseless flight, the *infinite* evasion of the Other: such is love's exclusive domain.

"Before love takes hold," writes Stendhal, "beauty is a necessary banner, promoting passion with the praise we hear others bestow on the object of our love." Nascent desire needs to be taken by the hand and reassured on its own account. The object of desire must be beautiful, and most importantly, others must accord it this supreme distinction. At first, Swann is astonished to discover a resemblance between Odette and Botticelli's portrait of Zephora from a fresco of the Sistine Chapel. It is as if the painting by the Florentine master validates the quality of his attachment. But passion breaks with Beauty, even though Beauty gave passion its start. Once won over by love, the subject gives up the visible and is interested in the face alone. It now matters little whether gossip and the needs of prestige justify his choice. He is liberated at once from Beauty and from conformity, no longer shackled by public opinion and its images that, in normal times, compelled him with irresistible fascination. This antisocial attitude or, better, this radical "agregarity" makes it legitimate to speak of someone "madly in love."

Be that as it may, the gaze re-aestheticizes itself proportionately as passion recedes. In the end, the Other becomes fixed in effigy, falling to the status of an image. When the fire is gone, situations are judged only by how they measure up to, or fall short of, the physical ideal to which the lover had once been so indifferent. The object, once literally lost from view, is now "unmasked," for if love is blind, its downfall hardens us in return, turning us into insatiable visual critics. The partner's weariness is no longer a distance that frightens us but a sudden sagging that blurs or ravages traits. When exhaustion takes over, the beloved face departs, leaving me there like "a reject,"[17] unable to contest this desertion in any way. On the contrary, weariness appears as a symptom on the face I no longer love: neither a flight nor a retreat, it is a visible mark.

And desire is once again prisoner of the spectacle it had successfully evaded. Once desire addressed itself to the face; now facial display will be its only target. The parentheses can close. Temporarily tossed aside by love, Beauty once again reascends its throne.

ALBERTINE ASLEEP

Two volumes of *Remembrance* are devoted to the relationship between the narrator and Albertine: *The Captive* and *The Fugitive*. The titles are misleading. *The Captive* recounts a flight, and *The Fugitive* tells the story of an imprisonment. An incarcerated Albertine continuously thwarts the surveillance of her jailer. Having vanished, Albertine imprisons the man she has left behind: everything he does focuses on her, and there is no escape from her inexorable absence. The prisoner is fleeting; the fugitive, captivating. In what then do feelings of love consist? In the impossibility of getting away from the one who perpetually gets away from you. Gone, the Other haunts you: a demanding phantom who possesses your soul and who, after taking the affection it is owed, leaves you to face the rest of your life with whatever tender feelings remain and a curiosity that is all but squelched. Though with you in moments of impulse, in devil-may-care times, the Other is never fully present, snatched away from your longing by an insistent distraction. Every experience, up to and including the greatest intimacy, is marked by the sense that the Other is not there. By setting other suitors aside, such *solitude à deux* promises to make the beloved face appear, but it obstinately refuses to appear. The marital bond fails to close this distance, only suppressing its incidental causes. For all this, anxiety, tenderness, and desire consist in "pursuing what is already present, in continuing to search for what one has already found,"[18] in "solliciting what ceaselessly escapes its form."[19] Simply put, in matters of love, presence is a form of absence.

Behind the play of facial appearances, changing expressions, and false pretenses deftly displayed, the alert observer can capture the essence of the face—"the music of the face," as Byron put it. The lover goes beyond appearances, only to bump up against the Other's perpetual evasiveness. With powerful attentiveness, the observer solves the enigma: the face betrays the person. Desire allows the lover access to its meaning: it is the face that effects the Other's constant departure and prevents the response to our call. Vainly, we seek to shore up the gaps, to enclose the object of our passion, to wall it in, to scrutinize its fundamental acts and gestures with searching, unflagging attention, thus placing it in a constant state of visibility—all for naught! The beloved face is not of this world, even when this world is a prison. Subjected to a permanent, exhaustive, omnipresent surveillance, the Other's eyes are the only means of evading the prison's hold:

If we thought that the eyes of such a girl were merely two glittering sequins of mica, we should not be athirst to know her and to unite her life to ours. But we sense that what shines in those reflecting discs is not due solely to their material composition; that it is, unknown to us, the dark shadows of the ideas that that person cherishes about the people and places she knows . . . and above all that it is she, with her desires, her sympathies, her revulsions, her obscure and incessant will.[20]

Sleep alone is able to conquer the Other's foreignness by lowering her lids, giving "her face that perfect continuity which is unbroken by the intrusion of eyes."[21] Albertine asleep provides the hero of *Remembrance* his fragile moments of respite. "Her personality was not constantly escaping, as when we talked, by the outlets of her unacknowledged thoughts and of her eyes. She had called back into herself everything of her that lay outside, had withdrawn, enclosed, reabsorbed herself into her body."[22] Sleep turns the face into a statue. With neither voice nor gaze, it finally submits to immobility. It remains the lover's task to trade his torment for contemplation and to take a rest from love.

Others will tell you the opposite: that their beloved's sleep stands as the moment of supreme distance and the most violent anxiety. That the sleeping face, far from submitting to their imperialistic greed, seems to bar them from the fantasy universe it allowed them to create. That in temporarily taking leave of life, the Other robs them of all influence. And finally that they have the hardest time resisting the imperialistic, ridiculous temptation of waking a partner who seems to have been unfaithful simply by giving in to night. The only compensation they discover for love's infliction of impotence upon them are those moments of utter clarity, when their eloquence casts a spell on the face of the beloved and captures it. Prouder and more jealous than Albertine's guardian, if such is possible, *they treat sleep as a rival*. They wish their word to be sovereign, and only grudgingly do they acknowledge that this power to enchant and hypnotize the Other must be shared.

Solace or abandonment: in fact, these two opposed reactions to confronting the sleeping face testify to the same mode of experiencing love. Nothing is more fluid, more uncertain, than the beloved face: another face always rises up behind the one the lover's vigilance has just grasped. Through voyeurism or seduction, such uncertainty—even if only for the moment—must be appeased. Both the alluring word that captures the gaze of the Other and the sleep that suppresses it immobilize the face, exhausting its inexhaustible well of absence.

TOGETHER, BUT NOT YET

I love you. You? Your good points? The brightness of your smile? Your graceful figure? Your fragility? Your personality? Your wonderful accomplishments, or simply the fact, miraculous in itself, of your existence? "It's not the person, but the qualities that we love," Pascal declares. "Does someone who loves another's beauty truly love? No, because small pox, which can kill beauty without killing the person, will put an end to that love." Conversely, according to Hegel, love means attributing a positive value to the being itself whom one loves, a value given independently of his acts or his unique and perishable gifts. Proust makes an original contribution to this venerable debate, contradicting everyone. Love is concerned with neither the person nor his characteristics, but aims at the enigma of the Other, his distance, his incognito, his way of always catching me off guard, even in our most intimate moments. The "you" of "I love you" is never precisely my equal or my contemporary, and "love" is the frantic investigation of this anachronism. It can be said, "according to a phrase that sums up equality, justice, the caress, communication, and transcendence—an admirable phrase of precision and grace, that [lovers] are 'together, but not yet.' "[23]

Love is that paradoxical bond that, as it deepens, strips the Other of every determination until she becomes impenetrable. As long as I was not in love with her, she was beautiful or ugly, nervous or calm, obsessive or hysterical: but none of these attributes can possibly sum her up now. I chose her for qualities that were wonderful, special, or unique; what I love about her now is not "a quality different from all others, but as the very quality of difference."[24] Passion silences everything adjectival: all the *this*es and *that*s that adorned the Other before love. Love's itinerary is a strange asceticism, a march toward the invisible that moves from qualities to the person and from the person to the face. Proust remarks that a novelist would be expressing an essential truth "if, while investing all the other dramatis personnae with distinct characters, he refrained from giving any to the beloved."[25]

Passion is neither a dream nor the novelistic form imposed on a trivial existence by an ardent soul. The lover strays, loses his head, acts like a drunken man in an altered state: but he is no lunatic. To love is not to ascribe sublime virtues to an ordinary person nor to decorate her with an illusory magic—for passion adds nothing to the beloved. On the contrary, love is subtractive; it lays her bare until that intolerable moment of insight when she surrenders "*as other,* that is, as that which does not reveal itself, as that which cannot be made thematic."[26] Unlike all those lukewarm emotions that go along with intelligence, passion puts us in contact with the abstraction of the face:

Springing from somewhere beyond our intellect, our curiosity about the woman we love overleaps the bounds of that woman's character, at which, even if we could stop, we probably never would. The object of our anxious investigation is something more basic than those details of character comparable to the tiny particles of epidermis whose varied combinations form the florid originality of human flesh.[27]

The lover gives up his prey for a shadow, knowledge for desire, awareness that pins down his object of desire and that fixes its place within a typology for an approach that experiences and sustains the Other's foreignness. When face to face with my beloved, she remains transcendent with respect to me. No information is gained by my proximity to her—because she never reveals herself as something in particular, never renounces her exteriority; nor is this a ruse. "This not knowing should not be understood as a *lack* of knowledge. It is not through a failure of understanding that love becomes love."[28] Love's communication transcends the alternative definitions of hallucination and revelation. The Other brings us more love (and suffering) than can be explained by the ideas we have of her, or by reveries conjured up in her absence.

Because passion is not an act of understanding, we categorize it as a kind of phantasm. Because the lover is not always clear-sighted, we say that he is out of his mind. If such is actually the case, his raving is less a form of losing touch with reality than an encounter with it: this sort of raving does not seek to obliterate the Other, as in ordinary psychosis, but rather to be overwhelmed by the Other. The terrible thing about love is the way it destroys all barriers, all protocol, all the conventions that keep human interactions on an even keel, that protect everyday life from the Other's face. In the state of love, the Other approaches you from without, sets up housekeeping within you, and remains foreign to you. It strikes you, until it monopolizes the entire field of your consciousness and slips away from your grasp. Irreducible to your analyses, refractory to your observational talents and your projections, the beloved face enters with you into an intrigue that resides outside the realm of knowledge, without actually descending into folly.

But we do not leave the world of representation without

a struggle. The shadow arouses a longing for the prey, and the lover's perpetually recurring uncertainties call out to us again and again, begging to be quelled by explanation. There can be no passion without the fight against passion, without the hope—at least momentarily—of returning to that lost paradise of clarity and revelation. We confide in those close to us, in friends we have in common. We frantically search for a sympathetic, willing third party to help us sort out the enigma. We recruit haphazard collaborators willing to join us in referring to the beloved face as "it." Is it favorable? Is it hostile? No definitive answer can be given to these questions, or so we suspect. The inquest closes with a dismissal. But these interminable, sterile exchanges produce nonetheless a real sense of relief. Things are said of the beloved. Her qualities have been laid bare. For a while, she has been weighed down with properties, dressed up with faults and strengths. I speak of her instead of talking to her or awaiting her address: even more than the substance and efficacy of conversation, it is this change in design that soothes my anxiety. Whatever the conclusions—optimistic or dark—commentary replaces the beloved face with a portrait, and the substitution is sweet. Put into words, the Other is like anyone else. We can *fill in* her difference: a difference that no longer incessantly disorients every idea I have of it.

It is not reason for hope or practical advice that I seek from such confidants, advice that is essentially useless: I ask them rather to join with me in the recuperation of the beloved. I want, in the instant of analysis, for the Other to return to the light and to subscribe to the general law of definition. In so doing, I do not progress beyond love, toward knowledge; I use knowledge to compensate for the characteristic dispossession that accompanies the state of love.

SUFFERING

It would be impossible to overstate the havoc brought about by the invasion of psychoanalytic terms into everyday language. Freud wanted to give humanity a clearer notion of itself; instead, our understanding of man is now obscured by Freudian clichés. Take the word *masochism,* when applied to the suffering of love. If your passion makes you insomnia's willing victim; if, in spite of every precaution, in spite of your powerful charms, the commentaries you heap upon her and the confidants you gather to your side, the Other escapes you: your acceptance of this humiliation of your intelligence means, according to the new wisdom of the world, that *you must have wanted it that way.* Your apparent sorrow masks a secret delight. Your plaint is a source of euphoria, and privation your version of plenitude. You are secretly satisfied, perhaps unconsciously, with what seems to do you harm. You realize your desire in affliction. The term *masochism,* which recognizes the central role suffering plays in passion, transforms it into pleasure. This turns love into one need among many, treats love's disarray as nothing more than a paradoxical (some would say pathological) form of its fulfillment.

But the suffering of love is not an underhanded way of being happy. And giving in to suffering does not mean finding pleasure in it but rather removing one's love life from the province of satisfaction. If, even while aspiring to serenity, the lover gives value to his suffering, it is not due to the surreptitious pleasures he enjoys; rather it is because his desire is not a *hunger* capable of satisfaction but an *approach* whose object always remains hidden. He knows, despite his complaints, that proximity to the Other is better than full and complete union. In this case, better does not mean more pleasant. The lover is neither sated nor for that matter unsatisfied: passion takes its chances with desire beyond the sphere of need, outside the alternation of frustration and contentment. Even when it is available, even when it is within reach of the caress, the beloved face *is missing,* and this absence is the *marvel* of alterity.

Present, the Other is always *next* (always yet to come, like a constantly postponed meeting). This is what plunges the lover into anxiety. His greeting of the sufferings "which had entered his soul like an invading horde"[29] simply acknowledges that restlessness is the truth of sentimental relationships. He is certainly nostalgic for idyllic times when he shared a common homeland with the Other, for a union that wards off the violent asymmetry between the beloved face and himself. But what is lazily called his masochism is, in fact, the refusal to give the idyllic the last word on love. It is here, perhaps—in this stubbornness—that the most profound wisdom offered by love's disarray resides.

Our vision of the ideal world is, to be sure, always idyllic. Beyond the infinite variety of their recipes, all social utopias pursue the same obstinate dream: to realize a communion in collective life as perfect as that of conjugal symbiosis. The new man, however constituted, is always given the task of shattering individual isolation: he is to put an end, once and for all—with outpourings of the heart or through fraternal combat—to solitude and separation. Instead of two incomplete beings joining together to form the harmonious entity of a couple in love, it is an entire society that merges in self-exaltation to form a single whole.

Today, the most recent of these grand utopias are under attack for their falsity, for using radiant visions of unity to disguise a horrible truth. But experience of the passions has taught us to contest the very beauty of this ideal and to deny this archetypal fusion its validity and prestige. Indeed, for such fusion to take place, for each being to be present to all, every face must be present to itself. In other words, the ever-elusive neighbor yields his place to this being shorn of mystery: the comrade. In this way, a community transparent to itself cancels the accursed split between the face and its manifestation, that split upon which suffering feeds. The "masochist" who loves does not give himself over to such happiness but withdraws the security of love from the fusional model. This is his wisdom: to denounce the idyll's eternal smile and the unlivable sweetness of a world without the Other.

THE ASCENDANT AND ITS HOLD

The lover seeks liberty but experiences oppression: such is the plot of most love stories we are told, from the most beautiful legends to the most saccharine novels. The antagonist who stands against passion in these age-old stories is the Law. The Law of duty—producing those agonizing inner conflicts, stirring strife between will and desire. The Law of repression: lovers defend their bond against the violent prejudice or rigidity of the social status quo. Or perhaps, in a recent update of this continuing scenario, it is desire that affirms its rights against the mutilations imposed by one-dimensional man. What we fear or approve of in love is the principle of opposing the Law, the power of transgression that defies custom, setting the intransigence of liberty against the combined forces of every power.

In this struggle, the Moderns take the side of individual liberty, while the Ancients take a stick to the caprices of desire, whether in the name of divine law or to defend the need for social cohesion. In so doing, both forget the essence of love and fail to recognize the ascendancy of the face, choosing instead to emphasize its quarrels with the censors. Such vicissitudes conceal the fundamental intrigue at work in love. The lover who (rightfully) defends his liberty against repressive authorities stakes his love upon and even sacrifices it to the idea of shared feeling. "Despite-me, for-another"[30]: to love, that supremely passive state, is to be exposed, in renouncing all shelter, to devote oneself, to submit oneself. Love means arriving at that point where there is no longer a lord and master. Love turns you into *the hostage of someone who is absent,* someone you cannot locate, nor elude, nor dismiss. This ascendancy is the lover's despair as well as his most precious treasure. It is both the violence he suffers and the value he affirms in himself.[31] Inconvenienced, practically obsessed with the thought of the Other, tired of waiting, this deposed king still prefers the fealty to which he has been reduced to his former position of mastery. And it is after this—after this subordination, after this passivity—that one languishes, in full self-possession, and dreams of experiencing love. At the end of *Remembrance,* Proust cites La Bruyère, who gives this paradox its most decisive formulation. "Men often want to love where they cannot hope to succeed; they seek their own undoing without being able to confront it, and, if I may put it thus, they are forced against their will to remain free."[32]

By pitting the exuberance of love against the inflexibility of the Law, we overlook this crucial fact: passion seeks to take the subject beyond liberty, without actually reducing it to slavery. "I am sick of loving," says the Song of Songs: this sickness is not alienation; this ascendancy is not oppressive. We experience this invasion of the self by the Other and should perceive it as absolutely opposed to domination. A nonliberty that is not a bad thing. Service that is not servitude. Passivity that is not a capitulation. This, the true scandal of love, amounts to much more than the violation of good manners or the transgression of norms.

Today we see the world as the theater in which a multifaceted conflict between liberty and the powers that be plays itself out. We conceive of a consciousness that is free or a consciousness enslaved, of independent subjects or subjects who are the prey of the Other. We even tend to think that, for the time being, independence is an illusion, that the freedom in which we think we live has been coopted by subtle forms of power. We are not the puppets of society, but we remain programmed by it. The system continues to mystify us long after we have stopped obeying it. In any case, the choice between autonomy and violence—actual or symbolic—exhausts our view of human reality. And so our goal is simple: to weaken the Other's ascendancy over consciousnesses. What then is love? A rude awakening, an anachronism in our modern world. The subject who loves does not recognize himself in any of the terms offered by these alternatives: the Other's presence within him is not alienation but an investiture. The lover's inner life is an offering, an uninterrupted devotion to the beloved face that liberates him from the burden of being free. This experience calls into question our unconditional privilege accorded to the confrontation between freedom and power. There must be a way to bow to the Other that is not subjugation.

This Other, to be sure, is only received to the detriment of all others. There is a single being you miss. Love may or may not be blind, but all those things that are not her are the first to go: the beloved face holds a facial monopoly. "When you love," says Proust, "you no longer love anyone." And Jouhandeau says, "Farewell to all faces. I will no longer recognize any but yours." Passion is a total repudiation of the world. Those who complain about being ignored are a nuisance: in seeking to survive their eclipse, they disturb a closed society, mad with love. Rivals are included among these bothersome people, but jealousy—so favored by the novel—is only the most dramatic and best known mode of excluding third parties. Jealousy is the blunt refusal that, in the name of the Other, is set against all others. The beloved face and the interlopers: this division defines the fanaticism of love, its virtual violence, its "ineffable iniquity," to use the phrase of one of Claudel's characters.[33] The experience of the Other nonetheless comes only at this price. Perhaps there is no other way, as Claudel puts it, of "making us understand our neighbor," of letting ourselves "enter into his flesh."[34] A secret affinity exists between the romantic consionsness and the moral consciousness, perceptible only if we tear ethics and passion from their own pathos, from that peremptory vision that unites them around the values of freedom and fusion.

Stranger and neighbor, he remains distant in his very proximity since his presence consists of always deferring his presence; he is close by at the moment of greatest distance. This being who flees me, who allows me no place of escape from him—such is the Other, in moral as well as amorous relationships.

EROS AND COMMUNICATION

On my bed, throughout the nights, I searched for my soul's loved one, I searched but did not find! Song of Songs

According to its traditional Jewish interpretation, the *Song of Songs* allegorizes the covenant between God and his people. Rabbis have succeeded in giving these overwhelmingly sensual verses an irreproachable theological or moral content. In the austere phrases of Lévinas, on the contrary, references to the state of love are inescapable. The notion of sexual liberation has taught us to regard intransigent terms such as *goodwill, responsibility,* and *bad conscience* with derision, while Lévinas impregnates them with an unexpected sweetness and violence. The fundamental ambiguity of Lévinas's philosophy allows it to be understood as an account of the affective as well as the ethical life. Sharply drawn descriptions of the encounter with one's neighbor inevitably recall the times of emotional duress the reader has had to endure, times so powerful, while they lasted, that normal life became impossible. The Other's face, obsessing and undefinable, finally evokes the memory or the presence of the beloved face; Lévinas's analyses comment quite naturally on the grand, passionate intrigues of *Remembrance of Things Past*.

There is nothing arbitrary in this fit. Lévinas begins his reflections on ethics with a phenomenology of pleasure. In the stages of his project, the carnal embrace stands as our initial confrontation with the neighbor; *eros* marks the situation in which the Other's alterity appears for the first time in its pure form. But the erotic is already an ethics. The lectures from the Collège Philosophique, collected and published in *Time and the Other*, already announce *Totality and Infinity* as if from the very moment when it seemed acceptable, even obligatory, to uncover the traces of sexual desire in each of our inclinations, even the most ethereal, Lévinas took the opposite tack. Finding not *eros* in *agape* but rather the shape of *agape* in *eros*, Lévinas searches our commerce in the flesh for a higher form of communication, a way of being in society that could not be reduced to survival of the fittest or to erotic union.

With Bataille and Sartre, Lévinas refuses to identify eroticism with sexuality. To speak of sexuality is to drive an effective wedge between intercourse and the rest of existence: we see it as need (more or less powerful, according to the season and the individual), analyze it as a function, classify it as one pleasure among many. But "voluptuousness is not a pleasure like others, because it is not solitary like eating or drinking."[35] The thematization of sexual instinct masks the fact that *eros* is relational, a doorway to the Other. Sartre turns this relationship into a version of the war between consciousnesses, while for Bataille it is the moment of co-incidence in which lovers break with the biological necessity that would force each being to remain distinct from the other: "The whole business of eroticism is to destroy the self-contained character of the participators as they are in their normal lives."[36]

In opposition to Bataille, Lévinas exalts the separation between beings that occurs when bodies meet. *Eros* is not the ephemeral theater in which the discontinuity between individuals is erased but rather the moment a vertiginous abyss is opened and explored. There is no such thing as *erotic* communion. Just the reverse. What desire discovers, and what pushes it to the verge of ecstasy, is the Other's indomitable *proximity:* stripped, submissive, swooning, the beloved withdraws more than ever from any relation to us. No escape: nothing about her relieves me of her alterity; under my caresses, her body *becomes nothing but face*. The maddest pleasure consists in not laying hold of anything; in ceaselessly approaching what one is not properly prepared to join; in beckoning, searching out, and probing an inaccessible flesh; not in vanquishing, in the happy confusion of union, the fateful necessity of distance and withdrawal into self.

The confrontational model is no more suited to carnal pleasure than is the model of fusion. Unlike Sartre, Lévinas discovers, in the insurmountable duality of the erotic relationship, not the battle maneuvers but the pathos of love, the actual pleasure of physical pleasure. To exist as two: I need every detail and all the fervor of romantic ritual to grasp the wonder this fact conceals. The Other is not an object I appropriate, nor a liberty that I must circumvent to affirm my own: it is a being whose mode of being consists in never completely giving in (to longing, to knowledge, to the gaze). What does it mean to make love? It is to pine away for one who is so close, as if, once all the obstacles have been raised—amidst the contact and the intertwining of skin—the Other still refuses to allow itself to be taken.

Before it is violence or violation, eroticism is the experience of the inviolability of the Other or, better still, of her *modesty* (*pudeur*). With a vigor all his own, Lévinas centers his phenomenology of physical pleasure around the term that signifies prude, *the ice princess:* the most pejorative term in our vocabulary for love. When embracing, it is useless to surrender oneself to the drunken pleasure of the notion that "all is permitted," to flout the laws of propriety in a thousand excessive, licentious ways, to violate each and every taboo, to abolish every last vestige of timidity or reserve, to sacrifice the chaste liturgy of normal conduct for an immodesty without bounds, for an unbridled savagery—it would not do: "the discovered does not lose its mystery in the discovery, the hidden is not disclosed, the night is not dispersed."[37] Lévinas gives the name *modesty* to this loss of light, to the impalpable reticence the Other sustains even in the depths of the most obscene nudity. Ravishing love deserves to be more than the state to which the discourse of liberation limits and finally reduces it: the victory of convulsion over convention.

The same is true for passion as for what once went by the name *concupiscence*. When I set out in search of a partner or my other half, I encounter the irreducible. I wanted a body that would yield itself to me, or a soul that would unite with my own; what I find, instead, is the obsessing proximity of a face. I wanted a perfect match; instead I experience an intraversable distance. I hoped to conquer and to possess, living "the possession—as if that were ever possible—of another person."[38] I believed, finally, that two join to become one. But the beloved being remains obstinately exterior. The relationship that links me to her "does not fill the abyss of separation; it confirms it."[39]

Does that mean, as Proust tells Emmanuel Berl, that love reveals our despair at the incommunicable? Is the fact that lovers fail to become one a sign of defeat? Is separation opposed to fusion, as the real is to the ideal, as the dark truth of the human condition is to the spineless embellishments of those unable to face it head on? Perhaps we should take our chances with the opposite idea: communication in love exists only as long as duality fails to transform itself into unity. As soon as the Other is no longer somewhere else, apart from me, as soon as she no longer surpasses my comprehension, communication is broken, and the erotic or passionate relationship fades into monologue.

In that way, the theme of solitude in Proust acquires a new meaning. Its occurrence resides in its turning into communication. Its despair is an inexhaustible source of hope. This is a paradoxical concept in a civilization that, in spite of the progress made since the Eleatics, sees in unity the very apotheosis of the being. But the most profound teaching of Proust — if poetry can be said to teach — consists in situating the real in a relation with that which forever remains other, with the Other as absence and mystery.[40]

3

Face and True Face

In all that he does, the lover affirms the value of his passion. He fights it off in moments of despair, from time to time makes the virile choice to regain self-control, lists for himself with implacable rigor all the reasons for giving up love altogether. But an inner voice "which lasts a little longer," as Barthes writes, "counter[s] whatever 'doesn't work' in love with the affirmation of what is worthwhile."[1] These periods of weakness are precisely what is worthwhile: the bouts of timidity, the powerless feeling. In short, love's defeats—seen as contemptible by the ego's military self-image—signal the presence of the Other. All our efforts must be lost for the Other to be revealed. Efforts lost: that is, to have lost the capacity to cast off or take back, to be unable to hold the beloved at arm's length, or to make the beloved square with our previous conceptions. To love is to enter into a relationship with a face that exists no more fully on the outside than within, that no more allows itself to be forgotten than it accepts being enclosed. You cannot close your door to the beloved, nor on the beloved.

Such is the double failure, a debt the lover owes because of his passion, as if his *stupor* and hospitality offered refuge from the *stupidity* of sovereign existence. Stupidity: that is, the condition of never being stupid, of always landing on his feet, his swift incorporation of any new face into the repertoire of established types and received ideas. Not a failure of thought, but thought's uninterrupted presence to itself, a serenity against which nothing and no one can prevail. Men speak; the parade goes by: stupidity is recognizable in the steady gait of a being undistracted and unaffected by words from the exterior. Not the opposite of intelligence, but that form of intellectuality that reduces all beings to its own level, that absorbs every beginning into a familiar plot. Nothing human is ever foreign to stupidity, and this is what constitutes, over and above ridicule, both its unshakeable force and potential ferocity.

"If I was the government I'd have all priests bled regularly once a month. Yes, Madame Lefrançois, a good, generous blood-letting once a month, in the interest of public well-being and sound morality." Now that's talking. And the immortal pharmacist of *Madame Bovary* continues: "My God is the God of Socrates, of Franklin, of Voltaire and of Beranger! I stand for the creed of the Vicaire savoyard and the immortal principles of '89. I have no use for any god who walks in his garden with his stick in his hand, entertains his friends in the bellies of whales, dies with a loud cry, and rises again after three days—all of them things which are not only absurd in themselves, but altogether contrary to the laws of the physical universe—which proves, by the way, that priests have always wallowed in slothful ignorance, and are for ever trying to drag down their flocks with them!"[2]

With this declaration, Homais sets himself up as the heir to the sages of the Enlightenment: the world is a theater of diametrically opposed forces. In the staged confrontation that ensues, he sides with philosophy against darkness, with reason against superstition and dogma. Homais pits the project of critical thought against Divine Revelation, which determines all in a single stroke. Like an adult who no longer believes in Santa Claus, Homais rejects biblical legend, the coin of the realm for a humanity still stuck in childhood. No authority can edify thought from without, for thought is no longer theology's handmaiden, having escaped the ancillary state to which the Middle Ages had tried to reduce it. Philosophy was born in Greece in revolt against the *doxa,* against public opinion; rejecting *orthodoxy* gave it birth, and Homais, the free thinker, turns this emancipatory movement into the source of his eloquence.

Father Bournisien, ignorant and sectarian, faces off against this calm, impious spokesman for modern times: their struggle symbolizes the schism between Science and Faith that divided nineteenth-century Europe.[3] The abbey knows but a single book—the one infused with the spirit; as for the pharmacist, he brandishes those books whose support for the spirit of critical reflection allowed thought to claim autonomy and criteria of its own. One figure wants to humiliate reason in the name of divine truth; the other wants to liberate man from revelation's truth and govern him according to the laws of careful, reasoned thought. And yet, these enemies are brothers: brothers in their obedience and in their reliance on received ideas. Though their values are contradictory, their gullibility is identical. From Bournisien to Homais, "the Absolute has merely been displaced, religion lodging it in heaven, liberal scientism placing it in human reason."[4]

The eighteenth century strove to free intellectual inquiry from the fetters of religious jurisdiction. In discouragement, the following century demonstrated the futility of such efforts. The struggle against obscurantism, the promised path to a new human maturity, produced nothing but a leadership switch. Reason, instead of placing Divine Revelation under assault by its destructive powers, hardened into the paralysis of revealed truth. Homais: a pious Voltairian and a devotee of science. His only response to the prejudices of the church: more stereotypes. One Bible replaces the other: the rationalism that treats scriptural tales as so many tall tales

produces a dogma all its own. No one thinks; everyone re-
cites: free thinkers and clerics are nothing but inert vessels
for the maxims of common wisdom. Nonthought rules everywhere, even in those systems of thought committed to
fight against it. Defeated in its religious substance, Revelation triumphs as a mental process. The name the nineteenth
century reserves for this universal catechism, this omnipres-
ence of the "readymade," is *stupidity:* "in one and the same
book, Flaubert shows us the odious stupidity of an anticler-
ical pharmacist and the odious stupidity of a priest who fully
justifies this anticlericalism."[5]

Despite their quarreling, the incredulous Homais and Father Bournisien share a secret solidarity that renders them
more and more alike: each believes in his idol with unconditional devotion. Both are malleable, since each adopts his
truths without the slightest inclination to think them
through, and both are unshakeable, since nothing new can
enter their minds. In short, both hold to a simple faith, and
this resemblance, called *stupidity,* annuls those oppositions
upon which the optimism of the Enlightenment had stood.

To mention "toeing the line" today, when discussing the
state of discourse in totalitarian countries, is to refer to this
Flaubertian model of stupidity. Like science, the revolution
has engendered its own Monsieur Homais. Imperturbable
and didactic, they recite their lessons, chanting slogans
learned by heart, proclaiming in an all but liturgical language
their steadfast loyalty to History's march. Their holy book
contains a maxim or proverb suitable for any event. With
the same aplomb, the same calm as the pharmacist, they
absorb each unique reality into the general, inflexible system
they keep close at hand. As soon as they begin to speak, we
know where they are headed: their words are simply varia-
tions, from a depleted repertoire, on a limited number of
themes. Science had hoped to defeat Faith: instead, it pro-

duced a catechism. Now, in turn, we apply a revolutionary critique that, having denounced religious alienation as the epitome of alienation itself, ossifies into a rhetoric to become "the monstrous Latin of a monstrous church."[6] Even when man believes himself to have broken with piety, he remains in its thrall. What is stupidity? The ironic revenge religious obscurantism takes on the discourse that sought to eradicate it: faith overflowing its own boundaries and insinuating itself everywhere.

Religious stupidity, bourgeois stupidity, revolutionary stupidity: at bottom, each follows the same routine. We obey rather than think; credulity wins out over the spirit of inquiry; instead of relying on reason, we prostrate ourselves before an indisputable revelation. Faced with stupidity's tenacity, the Moderns admit their defeat and proclaim their innocence. Reason has been unable to put an end to revelation's power over men. If nonunderstanding prevails in our world, it must hold on as a stubborn anachronism, not as the truth of an era that has labored as no other to break down every barrier to the intellectual independence of the thinking being. But the judgment remains a summary one. We cannot be sure that piety and obedience alone ossify the active intellect into stupidity.

The modern age was shaped as much by the advent of this crisis of consciousness as it was by reason's emancipation. The dissolution of *interiority* goes hand in hand with the critique of *authority*. The human subject takes the initiative, placing itself at the origin of society, knowledge, and law. No more divine right or truth: man establishes his sovereignty where the impenetrable wisdom of the Creator once reigned. But scarcely has man begun to grasp the distinctness of his reality, scarcely shaken off the bond of submission to the Almighty, when he finds himself cast into the chains of social conditioning. Man's control by exterior

forces comes to an end, but only as a new kind of subordination begins. Man is no longer his own master: he remains
oblivious of his true motives and acts without self-knowl-
edge. His consciousness's depths are illusory. The value of
his words lies not in what they say but in what they betray:
membership in society, unconscious desire, the logic of History. In the gap between what man is and what he knows,
the social sciences have established their kingdom; the discovery of this abyss has allowed knowledge to make great
strides. No one can deny the beneficial repercussions on the
individual and his life in society. By establishing psychic reality as a special field of investigation, by discovering what
evades the subject's conscious grasp, society gave itself the
means of rectifying, of redressing or anticipating phenomena over which it previously had no power.

But this widespread suspicion has produced a dogma all
its own. If credulity—whether militant, steadfast, or simply
conformist—truly consists of *listening without interpreting,*
there is another form of stupidity at work in political and
religious discourse, as well as in daily life. With all the trappings of discernment, this new form of stupidity carries the
charm of insight: *to interpret so as not to hear,* to flee from
spoken or written words into the unsaid to which they bear
witness, to dilute them with their context, to see the speaking subject as nothing but the discourse that speaks through
him, and thus to escape, in a kind of continuous defiance,
every cutting or disturbing edge a foreign word can possess.

To interpret so as not to hear: this form of nonunderstanding counters our received idea of stupidity. Stupidity
is neither passive nor bovine, but alert and busy, always on
the move. Mischievous, it rejects quantification, aware that
men do not originate their own speech. Such stupidity is
therefore careful to look beyond the literal meaning of spoken words to "a coherent Discourse to which the speaker

merely lends his tongue and lips."[7] By examining the speaker's social context, by infiltrating the web of connections that constitutes his discourse in order to grasp (better than the speaker himself) the secret motives and the true import of his words, this form of stupidity protects itself from actually discovering anything: any new meaning that emerges is nullified by a demystificatory subterfuge, rather than by faith. The Other does not speak; he is spoken: with the passive voice, the trick is turned. Nothing is said, at least in the gaps of discourse, beyond what the listener hoped to hear.

Rather than opposing thought directly, interpretive stupidity steals thought's tools, turning them around to assure its own victory. Systematized suspicion is effectively deafening: the paradoxical deafness caused by a superior ability to hear, with the glaring deafness never expected from one with so fine an ear. This is how stupidity, disguising itself as vigilance, spreads through the world with an indifference more determined than even M. Homais's. Those who practice such stupidity as a way of cutting off further discussion do not justify their action with transcendent authority and its status. Reading between their interlocutor's lines, or laying bare the directives that structure his life, they discover the hidden truth that determines him. In this face-off, they display not "the stubborn head of the man who hears nothing" but the wry smile of the man who hears *better*.[8] Their arrogance, and their droning repetition, claim the rock-solid alibi of a more profound understanding.

THE SURVIVOR'S PRIVILEGE

Obtuse, a blow-hard, smugly self-satisfied, resplendent in his stupidity: so Father Bournisien appears. When Emma Bovary comes to see him, paralyzed with confusion, he completely misses the quite obvious turmoil she is suffering. Is she ill? "The first warm days are terribly taxing, don't you find? But there, we are born to suffering, as St. Paul says."[9] His head crammed with maxims, the clergyman takes flight from the moment by retreating into his citations. Even more materialistic than M. Homais, he explains spiritual anxieties and heartaches by translating them into physical needs. The farce culminates as he delivers his *prescription* to the woman who had come searching for confession's clarity and peace. " 'Are you feeling unwell?' he asked, stepping forward with a worried expression: 'perhaps it's indigestion? You should go home, Madame Bovary, and drink a little tea. You'll find it very strengthening, or a glass of cold water with some sugar.' "[10]

Madame Bovary's experience is a common one: her words are spoken in vain. Distressingly useless, they shatter against her listener instead of becoming a part of him. In common parlance, we say "I'm talking to a wall" to describe the discouragement that grips us when we feel we are not being understood. Today, however, Madame Bovary would be taking a different chance, running the risk of being *absorbed* rather than *misunderstood*. "An hysterical petite-bourgeoise" Bournisien would think: part psychologist, and part clerical social worker, he would listen to her "story" and ask her, without seeming to delve too deeply, about her environs and her childhood. This able decipherer would then read between the lines of her statement, uncovering what she means to say or, more precisely, what she *does not* mean to say but says in spite of herself. Poor Emma's struggle would be less to make her words understood than to take them back. She would have the strange, painful, and revolting feeling of being defenseless and *voiceless,* even as she spoke, when confronted with the interpretation her story receives. Her feeling would be unlike speaking to a wall but like being walled in, eternally condemned to ratify a secret that always escapes her. And rather than trying to evoke a flicker of intelligence in the inanimate mass of her interlocutor, she would feel compelled to flee her own reification. In short, she would be enraged by the sight of her confessor proffering his verdicts as if he were her survivor. For there are two ways for thought to become sectarian and to cut its link with society: the necrotization, mummification, and petrification epitomized by Father Bournisien or, in opposite fashion, the objectification of the interlocutor, who is then fixed as the unique essence reflected in his words, denied the right to vindicate or flee the self-image that has been constructed. Narrow-minded thought on the one side, *mortifying* thought on the other: "The stupidity at issue here is not a mental condition; it is no less than the most dangerous of mental maladies because it threatens life itself."[11]

The wisdom of love: it is now possible to clarify the meaning—or at least one possible meaning—of this expression. The beloved exists in a state of what is effectively permanent resurrection. I decipher endlessly, but the beloved eludes enclosure, never coinciding perfectly with the devoted discourse, recoiling from each of my efforts to surround or encircle. Love, where all is forgotten, is a summons back to the Other: the enchanted dream calls upon consciousness to awaken to the irreducibility of the face. A sobering thought, this intoxicating evasion, for those who view it from their imperialist stance. Instead of being dealt with from on high, looked down upon by a panoramic gaze, or listened to with a suspicious ear, the Other is welcomed, with a hospitality that completes the metaphysical meaning of love.

This does not justify the conclusion that wisdom's necessary and sufficient criterion is to fall in love. But when the Other is met face to face, as in love, thought has a chance of discovering a new truth. When the Other is incorporated, thought repeats its own certainties ad nauseam and becomes, as Musil says, a threat to life.

Face and True Face

At the start of 1983, the Red Brigade's cell in Rome abducts Germana Stefanini, a sixty-seven-year-old prison guard. The perpetrators of the abduction immediately put their victim on trial before a Revolutionary Tribunal. In the apartment where she is held, the clandestine trial takes place, which concludes with Stefanini being sentenced to death for having carried out a "repressive function . . . at the expense of communist proletarian prisoners." She was executed on 27 January 1983.

The minutes of the trial were recorded on cassette. Here is an excerpt:

How is it that you became a guard at Rebbibia?

Because I no longer knew what I was going to live on. My father had just died.

Did you take a test?

No, I got in as a disabled person.

What did you do?

I distributed packages to the prisoners.

Stop bawling! Anyway, we don't give a damn. I'm telling you, stop, you're not getting any sympathy from us.[12]

The year 1983: the agony of terrorism, the end of a terrible period. This sordid murder shows the degenerate condition into which the Italian "armed struggle" had fallen. The Brigadists, who had defied the state during the Moro affair, avenged their friends held at Rebbibia by taking after an old, unknown, sick woman. A lamentable episode, but one that cannot simply be written off as another newspaper item. The execution of Germana Stefanini, this "logical crime," lays bare the essence of terrorism.[13] In it we see the weapons of criticism turned quite literally into blunt weapons, and suspicion blossoming into stupidity. The implaca-

bly coherent stupidity of this event stands as an extraordi-
narily rich contribution to the history of inhumanity in the
modern era.

"You're not getting any sympathy from us." Unlike the
placid Father Bournisien, the Brigadists' indifference in the
face of suffering results from their powers of insight, not
from cruelty or distraction: they know who Germana Stefanini is better than she does. The case becomes a matter of
who she is, which is to say, what position she occupies in
the social scheme. To be moved by her—in a kind of fatal
myopia—would have meant treating her as a unique individual, separating her case from the historic whole that gives
it meaning. "Stop bawling." Your hysteria is useless; it will
not distract us from the system that gives your existence its
true significance.

In the guise of a trial, a dialogue of the deaf joins the battle
between the terrorists and the accused. Bewildered, she pro-
tests her poverty. Gravely, they see only the position she
occupies in the society against which they revolt. She is a
victim but is treated like an executioner by her oppressors.
How can they, in good faith, invert a situation whose truth
screams out for all to hear? By pushing the process of interpretive reduction to its paroxysmic extreme: everyone is defined by his function and effectively cloistered in his class;
all faces disappear behind the principles they represent. A
more subtle Marxism would object to the transformation of
this poor, part-time prison worker into a soldier of capital.
But that is not the point: what connects these pitiful Brigadists to the grand revolutionary tradition is the way they
lock beings into their social identity.

From then on, the die is cast: Germana Stefanini can certainly tell her tale of woe, explain the absolutely innocuous
role she played in the prison. None of this will reach her
judges's ears. They inhabit a world where words say nothing,

only reflect something else. She is the mute manifestation of the social group to which she belongs. When Stefanini explains herself, it is the bourgeoisie that speaks. "What do you have to say in your defense?" they formally and scrupulously ask the accused, already condemned as the permanent symbol of her social identity, that is, of her guilt. They carry judicial terminology over into a context where language has disappeared, staging a confrontation simultaneously emptied of all reality. This is the essence of totalitarianism: not so much the trial as the fact that the very people compelled to appear are judged in absentia. A cursory or lazy reading of Kafka has turned the title of his most famous novel into the emblem of the totalitarian world. It is not the trial, not the exercise of justice, not even repression (in spite of all the pejorative connotations given this term by the leftist era) that defines institutional or clandestine terror, but exactly the opposite: such terror is the *duly and properly* executed destruction of law and of repressive justice. The humor—albeit involuntary—of totalitarianism consists in having chosen the solemn trappings of a trial in order to subvert justice, a humor that Kafka's novel describes with precision. Anyone who could turn a trial into the symbolic apotheosis of global control over the individual could not have gotten the joke.

Repressive justice, and repression without justice, are thereby conflated to become an identical object of opprobrium: in an awe-inspiring confusion, totalitarianism and its opposite become one. The accused respond when summoned, state their identity, plead their case or do not: but in a certain way, they are silent in spite of their words, and the trial unfolds in their absence. The court never, in fact, addresses them—the individuality of their being or the specificity of the act committed—but only the idea they represent. People are subjected to a human ceremony—the judicial ritual—only to be confined to their social sphere or their role, rigidified into symbols, treated as stand-ins for an evil power, like actors in a play performed over their heads, like people who no longer belong to the human race. They are men reduced to the state of monkeys, interrogated by a justice that has itself been reduced to protocol. How could they possibly speak in the first person; how could they be understood? Their interiority *means nothing;* their place, their answers, their function in historical time, are determined in advance, once and for all. Their existence springs not from the self but from their relation to a totality over which they have no control. With the social order inscribed in their brains, the substance of their lives consists in ratifying their essence, in playing their role to perfection. The verdict aims at just this behavior, inescapable whatever they do or say. In the totalitarian world, everyone is a potential defendant, and no one is up to the task of mounting a defense. Those called to trial are beings ontologically deprived of the possibility of responding. In a supreme irony, the floor is given to those who have from the start been deprived of the ability to speak. The observance of legal conventions goes hand in hand with the cancellation of any possible legality.

The murder of Germana Stefanini ratifies an erasure that has already taken place. The Red Brigades killed someone who did not exist, someone whom their stupidity had already suppressed by taking away her language and depriving her of her human shape.

THE UPROOTED VENETIAN

When, on 13 January 1898, Zola published his famous "J'accuse," Barrès, the most eminent of the anti-Dreyfusard theoreticians, was not particularly moved. "What kind of creature is this Monsieur Zola? Look at his roots: the man is not French."[14] The sincerity of the author of the *Rougon-Macquart* was not in doubt, but "there is a frontier between us. Which frontier? The Alps. . . . Émile Zola thinks quite naturally with the thoughts of an uprooted Venetian."[15] Barrès offered no reply to the evidence of Dreyfus's innocence, nor to the list of irregularities committed by the military during and after his trial. Did all this make him feel uneasy? Barrès was no more troubled by his adversary's arguments than the judges of Germana Stefanini were moved by her sobs: it was only natural that the part-time Rebbibia prison guard sounded like a capitalist running dog. Let Zola rage, denounce, and use implacable logic to unveil the weakness of the case against Dreyfus; let him deploy every last ounce of intelligence and style on behalf of his cause: his efforts would prove only that his alien linguistic origins lay in that anti-France of a thousand faces that imperiled the very foundations of the nation.

The differences, of course, between this prophet of fascism and those belated revolutionaries are both glaring and numerous. Barrès grounds the individual in his land, the Brigadists in his class. In the name of roots, the Brigadists glory in the determinism that bends humanity to its law: for Barrès, the past casts a decisive shadow on the contemporary life of each of us; no one escapes from inherited drives, the fate of his lineage. Nationalism is the exultant recognition of this slavery: "It is a true vertigo the individual plunges into only to find himself in his family, in his race, in his nation."[16] Prophets of a glorious future deplore humanity's scattering into contending social forces, calling it social conditioning or alienation. Committed to the abolition of class society and the end of all particularities, communism is nothing other than a promise of unification. Barrès is hostile to the very notion of man, whereas the Brigadists hope to create him. The only point of agreement between these two philosophies: human autonomy is a fiction today; man is not free but enveloped, inhabited, territorialized. Whether in the form of terrorism or history, a totality encompasses man and prescribes his behavior.

Does enlightened reason govern the world, or rather the dark power of the irrational, the mysterious ancestral presence that dwells within the soul of the living? Does instinct hold men in its hand, or does the impersonal logic of historical reason absorb them instead? A distinction without a difference. For each of these schools of thought, in fact, life's activities unfold outside the conscious control of the independent subject, and each reduces the individual to instrumental status, seeing man as a means of realizing a destiny that transcends him and that he unwittingly brings to pass. Destiny, which in one case goes by the name *reason,* in the other goes by the name *race.* For both, reason is no longer a human attribute: it is denied or shifted to history, but in any event it remains something of which living creatures have been deprived. "We are not the masters of the thoughts that are born in us . . . According to the milieu in which we are steeped, we elaborate judgments and deliberations."[17]

Conceived of as a being capable of reason, man is sovereign; conceived of as psychological subject, he is enslaved: we have already seen how this contradiction between liberty of the spirit and alienated consciousness has characterized the modern age. Totalitarian thought resolves the problem by simply disavowing the reasoning individual and casting him aside. Such modes of thought deny that the subject possesses any independent power, above all the power of the self to transcend its own history by an exercise of the cogito. Nothing in him—no faculty, no principle—keeps him from being completely historicized, from being reduced to a series of social behaviors, or to the unconscious directives of his country and its dead. Individual reason is absorbed into psyche, and the psyche is in turn gobbled up by the society, the tribe, or history. In short, there is no more logos in language, and the significance of a word resides not in what it says but in the site where it is uttered: words—once domesticated—do no more than express their provenance. "From where are you speaking?" is the totalitarian question par excellence. "From what context do you speak?" which is to say "who, when you think you are speaking, is speaking in you?"

FACE AND TRUE FACE

Germana Stefanini, before her judges, and Zola, in the eyes of his adversaries, are a little like the trees Francis Ponge describes in "The Cycle of the Seasons" and their pathetic and vain effort to accede to language:

Tired of having restrained themselves all winter, the trees suddenly take themselves for fools. They can stand it no longer: they let loose their words — a flood, a vomiting of green. They try to bring off a complete leafing of words. Oh well, too bad! It'll arrange itself any old way! In fact, it does arrange itself! No freedom whatever in leafing . . . They fling out all kinds of words, or so they think; fling out stems to hold still more words. "Our trunks," they say, "are there to shoulder it all." They try to hide, to get lost among each other. They think they can say everything, blanket the world with assorted words: but all they are saying is "trees."[18]

Zola seeks to persuade: his argument is imbued with the illusion that he is fighting for truth, that he is making a factually valid case with irreproachable logic. Actually, Barrès tells us, he is only showing his origins, speaking as a mouthpiece for his local god, a god who has possessed him from birth. Amidst her tears and stupor, Stefanini hopes to dispel the misunderstanding of her abduction and the trial that followed it. Her only message: that of capital. "You can't get

blood from a turnip": you cannot escape your ethnic or social ties with words or gestures that can never add up to
anything more than a series of ineluctable pleonasms.

Ponge sketches a beautifully fanciful, hypothetical world
in which trees strive to speak and can never succeed. In the
totalitarian world, on the contrary, it is men who, though
believing themselves to speak freely, can do nothing but unfold their leaves.

*Always the same leaf, always the same way of unfolding, the same
limits; leaves symmetrical to one another, symmetrically hung!
Try another leaf! The same! Once more! Still the same!*

Animal loquax: man alone is the speaking animal. Of
course, say the Brigadists and the anti-Dreyfusards who correct us, but man himself is a mirage: speech belongs to a
plant that takes itself to be man, to a tree that deludes itself
but is betrayed by its very chatter. In fact, we do not escape
the self in discourse but signal its presence; we never achieve
detachment, never elevate ourselves to the Olympian level
of ideas, but only expose our roots.

Man, you say? "What man?" Barrès immediately asks.
"Where does he live? When did he live?" Men exist only in
particular historical situations that their words lay bare.

Totalitarian thought can thus be defined as a thought that
succeeds in localizing the most abstract language in order to
reduce it. A thought that sees words as signifying only the
person who speaks them—that flattens the individual into
the collectivity in which it has been his fate to dwell, that
stops, *in the name of truth,* "the unclear and uncompleted
metamorphoses which the human face so miraculously expresses."[19] In a word, totalitarian thought sees the true face
beneath each face—ethnic or historical—and judges its
uniqueness and elusive mobility to be both a mask and betrayal.

The wisdom of love: the encounter with the face. Totalitarian stupidity: the unmasking of the true face. The face
speaks; the true face betrays itself; the face expresses itself,
"undoing at each moment the shape that it offers." The true
face is unmasked by its lies and its confessions, by its sincerity as well as by its deceptions. In its constant ability to
disavow the words it speaks, to use words to go back on its
word, the face calls what has already been said into question.
The true face cancels any possible question in advance: it is
the worm in the fruit and the perpetual avowal hidden at
the heart of denial. The face witnesses what it brings to appearance, which means that it escapes its own appearance by
correcting it, modifying it, constantly coming to its aid. The
true face, on the contrary, can only confirm its image, never
help it. In the first case, language suspends any definitive
classification. In the second, the word conceived as avowal
allows the Other to be categorized. It is probably apparent
by now that the true face is not the truth of the face but its
negation pure and simple. Perhaps the Other has the power
to refute what I discover in his soul, or perhaps he only
reveals the secret he possesses in spite of himself. Perhaps he
is foreign to me at first, or maybe he is at first foreign to
himself, and I am the master of his truth. True face: mastered
face, petrified face, a muzzled word, practically silent at the
very moment it is spoken.

4

Breaking the World's Spell

It is tempting to view totalitarian violence as the opposite of humanistic generosity. In the one case, to be sure, man—guilty from birth—is completely incapable of responding to accusations leveled against him; in the other, the individual's vile acts find absolution in the social context that forcibly produced them. While the totalitarian concept of *objective crime* allows individuals to be condemned for what they have not done, humanism excuses *actual crimes* by ascribing them to history or society. These two views of the human condition, however, share the belief that evil, when it occurs, is a result of faulty social organization. Things as they are wage a continual struggle against human potential, a struggle that gives rise to every vice and all the suffering with which humanity is so grievously afflicted. Blame is thus transferred from the individual to the system, giving us a glimpse of that time to come—a golden age—when, with the disappearance of a mistaken social order, being will finally come into its own, and Evil will be abolished.

In this view shared by humanism and terrorism alike, those who lag behind the times, who keep on blaming the individual for his mistakes—or for vexatious problems actually caused by a tyrannical social order—dance to the tune of appearances and the reactionary spirit. They are unable to link effect with cause or to connect a symptom with the illness it reveals. They turn a social problem into a fact of nature, thereby perpetuating the problem by denying it has a solution. Basically, they are near-sighted misanthropes.

Generosity and depth of insight, hope and clarity of vision, are nonetheless seen as joining hands to create an intellectual position insisting on the difference between man as a product of social conditioning and man as he is. This position distinguishes between alienated and liberated desire and attributes the miseries and failures of existence to those external forces that control man, desire, and life. Born good and free, we are predestined to pleasure and Good. If corruption or frustration show themselves within us, they do so only as the mark and trace of repressive power and social injustice.

A refusal to tie man down to the evil he commits or to the evil he is led to endure: such is the illuminating notion that leads humanism and terrorism to interpret rather than listen, to discover the insidious presence of conditioning lurking behind liberty's facade, to englobe the individual in the totality, and to reduce his word to what it masks. Because the society you have internalized is guilty, you are innocent: this sums up the credo of modern humanism.[1] Because the society you have internalized is guilty, you will have to disappear: the fundamental axiom of totalitarian thought. Whether treated as victims of the system or as its henchmen, men are no longer responsible: they are possessed. And what is more: absolute goodwill relieves total violence of its scruples by instructing it to see living persons as nothing but those forces that have conditioned them, as the order that imprisons them. To better celebrate man, man is stripped of responsibility for his acts and of the very materiality of his existence. Incontrovertible proof is given that man derives his meaning from a historical and therefore contingent social totality; his face is dissolved into the context in which it is inscribed. He is reduced to being one of power's capillaries, a power that terrorism, in its fashion, so expeditiously fights.

Terrorism? Fast-track humanism. It is a way of hastening the advent of civilization by liquidating the representatives of the old order.[2] No flesh and blood beings are targeted but the bourgeoisie or capitalism—that is to say, the system that inhabits and manipulates man. Through this double sublimation—of homicide into the birth of the new, and of the person into abstract entity (the true face)—the very consciousness of having committed a crime is erased.

A RADICAL ATHEISM

Imagine responsibility at the moment when the aspiring heart and a sober refusal to be fooled join forces to argue for human irresponsibility; define the subject by his resistance to conditioning, instead of excusing him by chaining him to a determinism of which he is unaware; remove him from the whole, instead of lumping him together with it so as to offer him fuller absolution; affirm that he has a destiny of his own, against the benevolent demystification capable of uncovering, in all human life, its "participation in mysterious designs in which one figures or which one prefigures"[3]; give man back his power to rise above his social context, to break with the system that fixes his place and being; oppose, in short, ethical reflection and the exculpation of man that passes for humanism today: this is certainly one of the most decisively innovative aspects of Emmanuel Lévinas's philosophy. By saying, in effect, that the subject, though part of a whole, exists as a separate being and derives his being from within, Lévinas's thought rests uneasily on what the modern age calls *morality* and *enlightenment*. It is the site of an invaluable slippage, allowing us to address the totalitarian experience in a language not its own and to confront that experience with something other than its own means or values.

This other language, the source of Lévinas's contemporary relevance, also marks what is most archaic in his philosophy. Our situation, in fact, makes it seem as if the author of *Totality and Infinity* were advancing, here and now, a philosophy of worldly demystification, as if Lévinas inherited it from Jewish wisdom and its rejection of idolatrous cults. In Judaism (this is the underlying meaning of revelation) *God speaks to man instead of speaking within him.* God raises man to the level of interlocutor and, like a teacher to his student, addresses him in order to tell him what he does not yet know and what he cannot discover on his own. Thus it is not the theme of a single God that constitutes the essential message of Judaism but the interval between God and his creatures. The Bible introduces the idea of *separation,* rather than the idea some still wish to see as the essence of religious life, the *communion* between man and the divine: "for his glory as a moral God and for the glory of the man who has come of age, God is powerless."[4] Religion's opponent is not unbelief as much as it is trances, devotion, or possession, all the forms of religious spirituality that can celebrate God only by denying man's dignity as a speaking subject and responsible being.

The numinous or the Sacred envelops and transports man beyond his powers and wishes, but a true liberty takes offense at this uncontrollable surplus. The numinous annuls the links between persons by making beings participate, albeit ecstatically, in a drama not brought about willingly by them, an order in which they founder. This somehow sacramental power of the Divine seems to Judaism to offend human freedom and to be contrary to the education of man, which remains actions of a free being. Not that liberty is an end in itself, but it does remain the condition for any value man may attain. The Sacred that envelops and transports me is a form of violence.[5]

A paradoxical religion, Judaism disenchants and desacralizes the world: God no longer inhabits beings or things in order to transfigure them. He has deserted the earth, taken leave of the tangible domiciles and carnal dwellings that paganism had sought to give him. What does the rejection of idolatry mean? To struggle against contamination, keep categories separate, celebrate the divine only after denying him "in the glamourous areas of myth and enthusiasm"[6]; in short, *to free man from God*. By substituting revelation (God speaking to man) for possession (God speaking in man), Judaism gives atheism a spiritual life.

The rigorous affirmation of human independence, of its intelligent presence to an intelligible reality, the destruction of the numinous concept of the Sacred, entail the risk of atheism. That risk must be run. Only through it can man be raised to the spiritual notion of the Transcendent. . . . it is a great glory of God to have created a being capable of seeking Him or hearing Him from afar, having experienced separation and atheism.[7]

Atheism and beyond: Judaism does not deny God's existence but rather claims man's existence outside of God. Bestowed with an initiative all its own, creaturely life breaks away from its creator and is able to forget transcendence and ignore the divine word. To put it more crudely, through revelation, God entrusts man with his own destiny, with all the risks and perils this entails: "If you testify to me, then I am God, and not otherwise—thus the master of the Kabbala lets the God of love declare."[8] Not only is man free from God, but the Almighty's very capacity to manifest himself depends upon man. Every human failing, as another text of Jewish mysticism puts it, causes the divine presence to retreat a bit more. And who is the first one in the Bible who contests this overwhelming fact? Cain, when he cries out after killing Abel, "Am I my brother's keeper?" With these words, Talmudic exegesis teaches us, Cain, the wily defendant, proclaims his faith: "I am not my brother's keeper, it's

You, You the Father of us both, who gave me the Wicked Turn, and who didn't put a stop, though you could have, to my criminal act." Conclusion: God has only his will to blame, or his lack of attention to Cain's crime; he is the true assassin.

Cain rejects the idea of separation in order to escape judgment. To better assuage his guilt, he unifies the human with the divine, according the Eternal One absolute power over the universe. The first murderer in history, he takes flight from the atheism of his condition in a religion that acquits man by alienating him from God. Cain thus appears as the inventor of both crime and mythology, and through him the Bible denounces not murderous violence alone but man's ever-present temptation to rely on the Almighty, to fall back on religion in order to lighten the burden of bearing existence on one's own.

Lévinas's philosophy fights this very same temptation, this same religion, when he defines *psychism* as the power granted each person to break the bonds of connectedness. Unlike modern thought (whose sources are mostly to be found in Cain's logic), he once again sees human interiority and the irreducibility of the human being as part and parcel of the power they obey. "The dimension of the psychism opens under the force of the resistance a being opposes to its totalization; it is the feat of radical separation."[9] To put it another way, the soul is not that realm of the self that is in principle capable of escaping the subject, but on the contrary, a form of self-relatedness, a mode of breaking with society or history. Lévinas gives the name *atheism* to this independence that allows the subject to speak (without immediately testifying to the totality whence he comes) and to think or more precisely to open the self to a truth from without: "One can call atheism this separation so complete that the separated being maintains itself in existence all by itself, without participating in the Being from which it is separated."[10]

To bear existence absolutely alone: the greater part of modern thought, in its dual concern with critical insight and humanity, refuses to grant man precisely this capacity. This mode of thought holds it as self-evident that man, an adult in name only, lives under the influence: freed from religious control, only to find himself enveloped by a destiny he cannot change, transported into a drama that unfolds without his knowledge. Modern man is not atheistic but inhabited. He is not his brother's keeper but the effect of his environment or the victim of his drives. If God has stopped giving him orders, it does not mean that celestial authority has yielded to human independence: such withdrawal is rather the sign of the sacred, signaling an opportunity for human beings to participate in the social order that has become their abyss:

That is what sorcery is: the modern world; nothing is identical to itself; no one is identical to himself; nothing gets said for no word has its own meaning; all speech is a magical whisper; no one listens to what you say; everyone suspects behind your words a not-said, a conditioning, an ideology.[11]

As a Jewish philosopher, Lévinas has no intention of authorizing a school of thought that shouts "God is dead" to the beyond, to the world's hope for consolation to come, to a world that is unsure whether such news is an occasion to rejoice or despair. It is not faith but atheism that Lévinas has sought to reintroduce to the world. His object is not to ameliorate the absence of anything sacred in our crisis-ridden age but rather to rid the world of the sacred, to empty Cain's discourse in order to return the word to the word, and autonomy to man.

Breaking the World's Spell

A VERSION OF JUDAISM

"God speaks, and man speaks to him. This is the great feat of Israel."[12] Even in our godless world, this fact retains all of its sacrilegious power. For the sacred has invaded modern thought in the guise of secularization and militant impiety. The heavens may be empty forevermore, but man is saturated by occult forces, foreign powers. He is not autonomous and can only mistakenly assert his claim to a distinct reality. His essential attributes are determined elsewhere: in actuality, he is defined by his historical situation, his inscription in a system, his participation in a totality. Man in the modern age is bewitched. His volubility itself is a form of aphasia. The only voice that speaks within him belongs to that imperious and unknown guest—the god—who has taken possession of his soul. "Nothing is said": the word is not free; it can no longer make a start, cut someone, reply, or instruct but can only confirm the implacable logic that secretly governs it. "Destroy the sacred groves—we understand now the purity of this apparent vandalism."[13] It becomes a question of whether man's power to act and to speak can be restored so that he is not seen as a product or reflection of that involuntary docility that destiny has prescribed.

Between the atheism of Jewish thought and a modernity that repudiates religious dogma, only to fall under the sacred's spell, a paradoxical and beautiful space remains. We would be happy to remain there if we could. But the Jewish God, infinitely distant and absolutely foreign, never fully vacates the void separating him from man. This God who speaks is also a God who intervenes. This God, who created a being able to bear witness as well as turn his back, often bends such human freedom to ends that his spirit's mercy, anger, or wisdom ordain. The idea of Providence, to put it

differently, is a Jewish idea as well, despite Jewish spirituality's avowed repugnance toward anything that might compromise the soul's self-presence, despite the pains Judaism
takes to establish that man is responsible for his acts. And
so, if Providence exists, we are justified and even required
to search for its traces, or its decrees, in great historical
events as well as in the most inconsequential human gestures. A controlling will pulls the strings and runs the game.
A coherent conception embraces and directs the human variety. The intrinsic significance of every fact also carries the
meaning given it by the divine scheme. Providence toys with
man, connects him to God, and takes control of his actions
by inscribing them in a master plan.

This enveloping and transporting force of the sacred is
violence: to challenge this violence is also to break with the
reading of the Bible it implies. One cannot hope to separate
man from God, remove him from his dependent condition,
elevate him to the dignity of responsibility, without saying
farewell to the tutelary image of the Almighty that Providence demands. The opposition that can resist the temptation to declare "Judaism is . . ."—as if Israel's tradition could
speak in a single voice and be summed up in a single definition—must therefore be a nuanced one. Judaism allows
two visions of the divine-human relation to exist side by
side: the religion of the Almighty and the religion of the
infinite. Either God resembles a Father in every way, and
our relation with him amounts, for all its lapses, to a recognition of his being, a fear inspired by his power, and a
faith in his protection; or, on the contrary, all that remains
of the God as Father image is the Creator who grants man
an independent existence, with all other figurations of the
Divine canceled in favor of this unfigurable idea of the Transcendent. He whom no definition can halt or enclose remains unnameable because to name him would defy the in-

terdiction against graven images, defy it by envisioning a God who would fill what should remain empty, approach what should remain distant, and bring the Completely Other within reach, turning the Other's mode of being into nothing more than a fantastical figment of our own reality. A good part of Jewish tradition is loath to speak of a Supreme Being because this seemingly superlative expression is fundamentally pejorative—in other words, it sells out the Absolute, the Ungraspable—in order to make it conform to the universal condition of being: "Each time that you attribute to God additional characteristics to God's essence, you assimilate him to the creaturely, you will be far from comprehending His reality."[14] We tame God, put him at our disposal, take back the distance separating us from him, and eventually denature him as we turn him into the head of the family or celebrate his effectiveness. To speak of Providence is thus to commit a double assault: against man, by nibbling away at his initiative, and against the Divine, by conjuring up his sanctity, that is, his radical foreignness. As Sartre wrote, involuntarily echoing a tradition he could not have known: "The absence of God is not some closing off—it is the opening of the infinite. The absence of God is greater than, is more divine than God."[15]

Lévinas himself makes use of Judaism's version of this intransigence when he places atheism at the center of his conception of the subject ("The soul, the dimension of the psychic, being an accomplishment of separation, is naturally atheist"[16]) but also when he applies religious categories to human relationships. Distant, foreign, transcendent, infinite: such is the face of the other man with respect to me. I accede to the theme of a radically other God through my impotence at dominating others. That "dimension of the divine opens forth from the human face"[17] to the very extent that the face, in fleeting transition, passes, exists, and imposes itself "in a manner unlike any other object in the world,"[18] escaping the idea I form of it and remaining unrepresentable. Lévinas's turn is not an expatriation of religion but the seizure and the transfer of religion's principle to the face-to-face encounter with the other, a new use of relations that usually describe God's relation to his creature.

THE TWENTIETH CENTURY

The contradiction between these two ideas of God—the Supreme Being and the Other—has never been more glaring, to be sure, than it is today. After two world wars, totalitarian governments of the right and the left, Hiroshima, the Gulags, the genocides of Auschwitz and Cambodia, it can no longer be a question of explaining such sorrow through sin, as faith has done for millennia.[19] No one could have visited such travails upon us: they represent nothing other than the scandal that they are, rendering the idea moot and above all odious that generations of the faithful have used to rekindle their ardor for God's rule over his creation:

If slander and libel is a great sin, how much greater is the sin of those who speak with looseness of tongue in reference to God, and describe Him by attributes which are far below Him.[20]

Henceforth we should say that when we talk of God, we are guilty of letting our tongues run wild *because* such talk is a way of diminishing the Other. By judging him as an existent among others, according to his effectiveness and his merits, by weighing him down him with words of praise, by envisioning him as frightful, imposing, powerful, and as our instructor, we do less offense to the Eternal One than we do to the victims of his care. There is not just an analogy between defaming our neighbor and adoring divine perfection: glorifying God is that superior form of defamation that gives useless suffering the seal of necessity. If God is, and if he realizes his being in history, if he reigns and if he is powerful, our century's great massacres are an expression of his will. Some logic redeems them, and a meaning attenuates their horror. They have served some purpose: to punish sinning peoples or to prepare for the world's redemption. Seen as evil from our finite, partial, and partisan point of view, they are—from the panoramic perspective of the Eternal—the necessary step toward a greater good, an indispensable moment in the accomplishment of his work. They possess a *raison d'être,* meaning that if they had not taken place, the world would be less perfect, less rational. Providence insults the murdered, defames their suffering by discovering that it contains a positive significance. "Each time that he heard the cliché repeated that the victims did not die in vain, he felt anger well up inside him" (Singer).

Is it chimerical, infantile, this image of God the Father? That it is, but not that alone. This infantile dream, this sweet, tenacious illusion that consists of adorning reality with traits of the paternal image, is also an unacceptable idea: henceforth Providence, not its dismissal, is unacceptable.

"If God does not exist," exclaimed Ivan Karamazov, "then everything is permissible." He was wrong. If God does not exist, if our century has robbed him of being's attributes, if we hesitate to say, "God wished, God chose, God ordered," and to speak of God as we do a doctor or a mother-in-law, it is precisely so that all is not justifiable, and so that suffering remains foreign to the principle of reason.[21]

THE SOLIDARITY OF THE SHAKEN

It is a great loss for man, that which he suffers when he has lost his belief in an all-knowing being who directs the world's course. Lichtenberg

Do not, however, underestimate Providence's power and attractiveness as an idea: it is more difficult than one might think to rid reality of any analogy to the Father figure. God is dead, perhaps, but only to be reborn immediately in other forms. No sooner had he disappeared than were his replacements at hand. The modern world has turned to History and Progress for an explanation of the calamities that afflicted it, in order to see those afflictions as regrettable but necessary stages in the realization of Good. Both of these grand secular divinities acquitted themselves of their task by replacing God's supernatural bounty with an immanent, invisible goodwill at work in the world. Whether in revolutionary or bourgeois form, progressivism has taken the baton from theodicy and has, with admirable energy, done its best not to leave humanity at loose ends.

These substitute providences are, in turn, contested. They are going through a difficult period, what is generally known as the crisis of values or the end of ideology. History and Progress have been carried off by the disillusionment that has accompanied our century's end. No one would declare today, as Merleau-Ponty did after the Liberation, that human history is a "totality moving toward a privileged state which gives the whole its meaning."[22] This notion of a history inevitably headed straight for its apotheosis has not withstood the crimes and countless atrocities committed in the name of its fascinating image.

Amidst this melancholy climate of farewell to modernity's aspirations, a spectacular renaissance of religious sentiment is beginning to take hold on all sides. It is as if humanity, in horror of its own emptiness, fearful of being orphaned, were returning to its original Father, after the interregnum of substitute absolutes. History follows God; God follows his successor: thus the providential throne never lies empty. And whereas we once attributed barbarity and fanaticism to the survival of spiritual fervor, it is on the contrary the decline of faith that is more and more often being called to account for every atrocity. What we took to be evil's cause (submission to the sacred word) is held up as its remedy: the obstacle becomes the escape, and we search the current revival of piety for assurance that God is alive and that he has not abandoned humanity.

There are those who connect this return to religion with the recent interest in Lévinas. When unbelief dominated thought, they say, no one read this philosopher: his partiality for God brought smiles. Now that God's prerogatives have been reestablished, we eagerly discover Lévinas and his work. If this is truly the case, then Lévinas is the victim of a major misunderstanding. When confronted by all the Doctor Panglosses whom no abomination can knock from the saddle and who unflappably affirm that everything that is must be, since God or History wished it so, Lévinas is more a partisan of Voltaire's. Nothing can bring the author of "Poème sur le désastre de Lisbonne" to resign the dead to the balance sheet of divine justice. When forty-five thousand people perish in an earthquake, their suffering is useless and not "the effect of the eternal laws of a free and good God that necessitate the choice." Lévinas radicalizes this position by questioning, in the name of victims of a powerful will, the idea that such a will could be the instrument of Providence or Reason.

A sign among so many others that the true divide, the fundamental split, is no longer between believers and free thinkers but between those who can still conjure a father for themselves and those who, to use the expression of the Czech philosopher Ian Patocka, comprise *the shaken,* "those who have experienced the shock, those who are able to understand what is actually at work in life and in death and, therefore, in history."[23] To them, the future promises nothing. The wars of the twentieth century constitute an experience too profound for them to fall for promises once more, whether those promises be lay or religious. If they are believers, it is in a faith more difficult than it was in the past, more uneasy, without guarantee, without theodicy. If they are not believers, they do not found cults to other forms of Providence or assume a God's eye view of the world. Both are condemned to the absence of rest: together they must mourn the Father, mourn the credulous piety that chalked human sorrow up to divine punishment; together they must mourn the simple atheism that celebrated the uninterrupted progress of humanity, discerned a rational principle in the course of events, an irrefutable coherence, and delight in knowing that Good was going to triumph through the very laws of history or nature. Reason withdraws from history. A similar uncertainty strikes divine presence and the idea of progress.

Pitted against these new modalities of religion and unbelief are necessity's confidants, those initiates in whom the stage manager confided the secret of his intentions, those who, caught in "God's gullet"[24] or one or another of his avatars, offer a justification for all. Men of faith or men of knowledge, nothing human troubles their monologue: for them, man originates neither his actions nor words. The world is not made up of people but of roles that each being plays from moment to moment on command from a higher will made up of true faces, from which no face can escape. Nor does anything inhuman faze them, since all suffering is part of the order, conforms to the grand scheme they describe with self-assured fervor.

5

The Test of the Neighbor

We have long identified moral concern with humankind's necessary liberation. What did it mean, what does it mean today, to love humanity, if not to forgive the atrocities humanity has committed by denying that humankind bears any responsibility for the conditioning that has brought it to this pass? Oppressed, therefore wicked: liberation from oppression is enough to enable us to seize evil by the throat. The deeper the individual's alienation becomes, the more the realms of Good and Liberty confound themselves into a single hope. Good is liberation's ultimate goal, and liberation is the condition that creates the possibility of Good.

In the meantime, Evil holds sway, and man is pure and innocent—*objectively* innocent. His faults are proof enough of his alienation. His egotism blames the pitiless universe from which he has sprung, and man's crimes are proof only of his enslavement. True, he acts, but his actions do not originate within: they are produced by the totality in which he is inscribed, a totality that makes him what he is. His behavior is dictated by laws that can be discovered through sociological analysis and that satisfy his heart's aspirations. Generosity and the powers of critical insight batten on one another in philosophies of liberation, instead of entering into conflict: a universal pardon is granted as a reward of the will to knowledge, and complete absolution for all faults is practiced in enlightenment's name.

Traditionally, knowledge disabuses goodwill of its innocence, serving as a counterweight by offering innumerable testimonies that confirm the villainy of men. But to water down the human condition until it becomes the social condition is to deny the existence of the reality principle itself. It is no longer the real that stands in opposition to the ideal, but the system. The fact that man is frequently prey to base desires says nothing about man, but everything about society. Those whom history has chosen to perpetuate this system, to consolidate society's power, are not truly responsible since they have no control, even verbal, over their own destiny. But here they are, saddled with a new and immense form of guilt: obstacles, as they go about their business, to humanity's liberation. The objective innocence of man presupposes the objective crime of class, of the group, or of the nation that keeps man from reclaiming his innocence. For members of this accursed collectivity, a social determinism of attenuating circumstances becomes proof for the prosecution. Instead of being excused, they are condemned by their social ties, even when their personal conduct might be irreproachable.

And so the notion of objective crime—the twentieth century's juridical innovation—can only be repudiated by simultaneously questioning the noble idea of objective innocence. In other words, to be antitotalitarian, philosophy must think of man beyond the totality: not as someone to be liberated but as someone already free. As independent and responsible, regardless of the limits his background might impose. Not determined, Lévinas will say, but *created*.

Creation ex nihilo *breaks with system, posits a being outside of every system, that is, there where its freedom is possible. Creation leaves to the creature a trace of dependence, but it is an unparalleled dependence; the dependent being draws from this exceptional dependence, from this relationship, its very dependence, its exteriority to the system.*[1]

86

What is a creature? A being who cannot be deduced from the social context or structure in which he was born. An existence springing from the Other, but in which the Other does not reside. An apparition that is not an emanation, that is, one that escapes the very thing that produced it. Situated in his time, molded by history, the subject exists no less *distinctly:* the concept of creation, instead of supposing men to be alienated, credits them with an inalienable independence. Only they, and what is within them, are asked to answer for their actions. Whether it absolves or condemns them, their conduct cannot be completely ascribed to the heredity that determines it or the context in which it is played out. This school of thought has no conception of objective crime nor objective innocence, just attributable faults.

We no longer are of an age when fairy tales suffice, and we have known for some time now that the world was not born of nothingness, in a single stroke through the miracle of divine will. The naiveté of this discovery, however, should not be overlooked. "In the beginning, God created heaven and earth": the power of this idea is not exhausted in the miracle it recounts. This story's force consists in distinguishing—by separating them in an irrevocable manner—the creator from the creature. Nor has this message, as conveyed to us by monotheism, fallen to the status of an anachronism. Just the opposite is the case: we moderns have demystified the golden legend of the creation. But by dispossessing individuals of their interiority, by conflating them with a totality from which they derive all their meaning, we have, in a way, regressed to a point where the idea of creation *ex nihilo* makes sense. It is to this idea we must return once more to disenchant the world and to trade the idea of a free—that is, separate—man for a vision of humanity possessed by the demons of race or by historical reason.[2]

Despite its surface appearance, Lévinas's work is no harbinger of a return to moral concerns. Nor is it a sign of idealism's revenge on a materialism that has held sway in recent thought, a materialism that viewed the human adventure as political through and through. For what distinguishes such philosophies of liberation is the disproportion between their ethical ambition and the absolute idealism they profess. They promise men a royal road leading to happiness, maturity, and the conquest of Evil. And because, for these philosophies, everything is political, skeptics who oppose their dreams with the recalcitrant contradictions of reality are immediately viewed as the dupes or, even more degradingly, as the advocates of the status quo. To speak of difficult liberty is thus not to reassert the moral dimension per se but rather to break with the morality inherent in all forms of discourse that abolish human autonomy in the name of a future freedom.

REALISM'S OBJECTION

Thus the individual is not reducible to the forces that engendered him, whatever they might be. But Lévinas's thought ventures beyond this thesis of separation, extending to the social life of this being who stands apart in the twin categories of religion and emotional love. The entire vocabulary used to describe the face-to-face encounter with the other man is drawn from the lexicons of theology or of passion. One can thus legitimately wonder if Lévinas, proponent of the separated man, shares a blindness to *man as he is* with those who expound the thesis of human alienation. It is no doubt intellectually invigorating to see religious categories brought down to earth, cleansed of any reference to the world beyond. But by transferring to human relations those principles that are valid only for relations with God, have we replaced one figment with another—substituted moral illusions for religious ones? Have we replaced simple piety with the wish to be pious? Since when does man regard the other man as a god?

Does the implicit but intricate parallel between ethics and passion haunting Lévinas's thought seem a bit seductive, not to mention unlikely? Men do not feel brotherly love for one another: no natural affinity unites them. Who still believes in the possibility of noble ideals? Who does not see them as a farce, a hypocritical screen behind which each man, even if he does not happen to give in fully to his worst impulses, is always looking out for his own self-interest, guided by nothing but the commands of self-interest? "Thou shalt love thy neighbor as thyself": a touching exhortation that is powerless in the face of rampant possessiveness and the drive to succeed. Man is not a moral being: now that dreams of total liberation are on the wane or, more accurately, are turning to nightmares, we are less inclined to consider this natural blemish an historical or social vice. An entire philosophical tradition that spans Hobbs to Adam Smith, overshadowed by progressivism, once again stirs in our memory. Its guiding impulse: the desire to found social life on a *realistic* basis. Realistic, which is to say, *not moralistic:* a school of thought responding to what men are, rather than to what they ought to be, grounded in our egoistical instincts, rather than in the virtuous injunctions that condemn them. Giving our personal preoccupations and mundane aspirations their due, rather than stigmatizing and seeking to heal us of them. Civilizing our destructive outbursts with other, equally spontaneous drives (the profit motive, the fear of violent death), rather than opposing all human depravity with the hapless religious precepts of devotion or humility. The wisdom of love? Just the reverse: for realism, wisdom consists in mourning love and giving up on this indefinable quality by replacing it with less beautiful, but more effective, passions as a way of making peace possible among men.

Moralizers turn love into a cure for evil; liberators see it as the goal humanity will reach after bringing its long hibernation in prehistory to an end. Realism asks us to learn to do without love's impracticality and to reject it as a goal we can never reach. In short, to be a realist is to compromise with human nature instead of condemning it, as some are wont to do; instead of claiming to correct it with edifying speeches or denying it pure and simple, as others do, by imputing all human vices in their entirety to a kind of social misfire. It is correct to say that Lévinas is neither a moralizer nor a liberator. In his work, love is no more a panacea than a promise. Realists will counter that by postulating relations of love or religion as ethical subjectivity, he is dreaming: " 'Man is wolflike toward other men': who would have the courage, when faced with the lessons of life and history, to line up against this adage?"[3]

IN A SENSE, NOTHING
IS MORE ENCUMBERING
THAN THE NEIGHBOR

Appearances to the contrary, Lévinas is no philosopher of altruism. His thought bears no trace of the natural goodwill that, in pity or generosity's name, inevitably brings us to help our brother or at least identify with his distress: to share, as if it were our own, the violence he endures. Lévinas offers no hymns to an instinctive sense of the divine, those sweet outpourings of the heart that could be construed as the reassuring testimony of our ethical vocation. There is no emoting over the original tenderness we bear toward our fellow human beings, no sentimental blather offered in place of the rigor of the law. Calculating self-interest, *conatus es-*

sendi, an imperialistic self pursuing its own agenda without compunction or concern, claiming its place in the sun: when it comes to describing the human being or, more precisely, the play of being in man, Lévinas borrows his concepts and even his vocabulary from Pascal, Hobbes, and Spinoza— divergent philosophers, to be sure, but thinkers who confronted the shock of dynastic and religious wars that had just bloodied Europe and who shared a common refusal to grant human morality any credit. Lévinas's thought certainly contains a moral theory, but not a morality of sentiment, with its predilection for redeeming man by making sympathy one of his natural affections. The same philosopher who constructs his ethics on the model of love also maintains a completely disenchanted vision of man as he is: that of Pascal, in fact, when he denounces the self because "it makes itself the centre of everything" and it "would like to be the tyrant of all others."[4]

The meaning of moral intrigue is summed up effectively in this paradox: morality, my morality, does not originate with me. My own free will does not choose to set aside the governing principle of all my actions—both good and bad— so that I act with the good of others in mind. Spontaneously, I live. To live: meaning you can exert yourself or just as easily save yourself the trouble; look for what is easiest or long for power; hold your strength in check or, on the contrary, let it run wild. In any case, the opening to the other is never described as a basic given, as an instinct I possess as part of my spontaneity as a living being. In other words, morality is a transformation whose principle is exterior to me. Properly speaking, a conversion. Something foreign—the face of the other man—intervenes, compelling me to interrupt my indifference. I am disturbed, disillusioned with my life, awakened from my dogmatic sleep, expelled from the kingdom of my innocence, and summoned by the other's intrusion to a responsibility I have neither chosen nor desired. Thus the realists are right about the morality of sentiment: ethical behavior does not come naturally. But they are mistaken to conclude that it is illusory or unreal. Ethics is my nature called into question by the face of the Other. I do not desire Good in the same way I might want pleasure or my own best interest: concern for the other seizes me in spite of myself, as if I were traumatized. The Other (and this is no doubt the very definition of alterity) announces the divorce between the human and human nature in me: because of him, I can no longer exist naturally.

Love thy neighbor? No, if you understand love as part of an enlightened philosophy of altruism, with its innate sympathy of man for suffering man. Yes, if the unctuous and insipid word *love* can still possibly allow us to perceive the weighty, overwhelming, obsessive proximity—the accusatory pressure, the kind of violence, the persecution—that my neighbor exercises over me. I cannot free myself of this Other from whom I am separated and who escapes my power. He makes it impossible for me to exist naively and fully, whether in the hedonistic lifestyle of a self who lives for pleasure, or as a heroic self displaying his power, or as a bourgeois individual dedicated to the pursuit of his own interests. The Other: the barrier to being. Here I am, forced to answer for him, weakened, beset with a moral obligation I do not wish to bear. I do not naturally love my neighbor; it is my neighbor who encumbers me, haunts me, crushes me—in short, who does violence to my nature by demanding my love.

In an approach I am first a servant of a neighbor, already late and guilty for being late. I am as it were ordered from the outside, traumatically commanded, without interiorizing by representation and concepts the authority that commands me. Without ask-

ing myself: What then is it to me? Where does he get his right to command? What have I done to be from the start in his debt?[5]

Man is not that peaceful being whose heart longs for love, depicted for us by those tender ethical systems based on sentiment. Love of neighbor is not inherent but imposed, like a duty from which man cannot hide "without showing the trace of his desertion."[6] The Other makes his appearance in the world in the imperative mode, and the love obligated by his presence carries all the pain that comes with renouncing a princely existence that indifferently takes its course. "Only a vulnerable self can love his neighbor."[7] Vulnerable, and not dynamic, scheming, or beaming: I am not the originator, throwing myself upon the other on a generous impulse; it is the Other who, entering without knocking, distracts my intentions and troubles my peace. Moral intrigue becomes insipid when we imagine the lover as playing the active role. The neighbor concerns me even before my heart or conscience has the chance to decide to love him. The face is that prescriptive force in him that deposes me from my sovereign position and forces a radical passivity upon me. Love, if you will, but unwilling love, a trying love: love, which is our most current name for the violence with which the Other dislodges me, claims me, pursues me into the recesses of my detachment. Hence the aggressiveness I can nurse toward this reckless character, this omnipresent absence, this *undesirable:* the neighbor; from whom springs, in a word, Evil.

Far from working as a veil of modesty, cast over humanity's fundamental beastliness and the crimes of human history, a love of neighbor sheds light on hatred for it precedes all. "Am I my brother's keeper?" Cain exclaims, and this excuse is, in fact, his confession, the very exposé of his motives. It is because I am not only my brother's brother (on the same plane as he) but also his keeper—his hostage, Lévinas ventures—that the temptation arises within me to have done with him, to break this unequal bond. Evil is revolt, the protest of a fallen sovereign—me—against the Other's unseating of him. From benign bad faith that uses every resource of the intellect to arrive at this clear-cut conclusion—"It isn't my problem!"—to exterminatory violence, Evil arises from an initial will to punish the Other for intruding on my existence. What is most detestable in the neighbor is not his role as rival but his face; not his supposed hostility, his menacing strength, but the command that signifies his exposure to me: "In front of the neighbor, I was in a state of comparison more than of appearance. I reply immediately to a summons. . . . But the responsibility to which I am exposed in a passivity such as this does not take hold of me like an interchangeable part, for no one here can take my place; by appealing to me as to an accused who will not be able to challenge the accusation, it obliges me as if I were irreplaceable and unique. As if chosen."[8] A chosen one, which is to say not someone who is privileged but someone who holds a position of responsibility, making me the object of an accusation even though I have committed no crime. This is what the face of the other man makes of me: my violence responds to the scandal of this selection.

It is clear: the meaning of the biblical term *chosen* is grounded in the relation with the Other. By calling me to him relentlessly, the neighbor selects me alone, me and only me: the me who has never said anything and who cannot slough off this burden onto someone else. Being chosen is a human modality before it is a religious category. To say so is not to exclude from consideration all that is ignoble in life but, on the contrary, is to give oneself a way to think it. Let us grant that, for all intents and purposes, man is wolflike toward other men. How do we account for this universal state of war? By instinct? By the indomitable fury that might possibly represent a persistent trace of our animality? By self-interest, the battle of egos clashing with one another? Such a response is tautological: man is violent because his passions are violent. In seeking to explain everything by Evil, realism is unable to imagine its birth. In short, realism is not realistic but simplistic: by conferring Evil with the status of a natural trait, realism evades the problems it poses. Thus, to put it accurately, human nature is not homicidal or barbaric; rather, it is the aspiration to return to those states that is barbaric. Faced with the Other, my life stands accused, my being is no longer mine by right. I am no longer at home in the world: an obligation appears that relegates the pleasurable duty of self-preservation or self-realization to secondary importance. The penalty paid by my existence is to be unable to find justification from within. Through Evil, I appeal this sentence, expressing both a resentment and the nostalgia its severity spawns. Nostalgia for a life, not more moral, but more organic, paying heed to its internal principle or movement alone. Nostalgia for vital energy and irresponsibility; the back-to-nature dream.

In the beginning there is violence, say the pessimists, those iconoclasts who have all but shed the illusion of human worth and who judge everything by its lowest common denominator. But disillusion is not always a measure of depth or truth: I do not hate another man spontaneously (nor do I hate him because I have been conditioned by an infernal, all-powerful system): I hate him for the irrefutable questioning of my spontaneity. I cannot forgive him for forcing me to make excuses to him.

"It is time," writes Lévinas, "the abusive confusion of foolishness with morality were denounced."[9] It is by contesting realism in its own terms, by implicitly denouncing *realism's foolishness,* that his philosophy succeeds in this act of rehabilitation.

The primordial given of man's relationship to the other man is not hostility but covenant or, in a language bereft of religious connotations, the nonpossibility of indifference. The Other concerns me before any decision of my own, changes the objects of my attention, takes me off the narrow path of self-interest against my will. Thus we must think of hostility as arising from covenant and not vice versa. Resentment does not, as Nietzsche would have it, result from the power of our love for others, that apology of the weak and unhappy. It is love, the neighbor taking hold of us, an ineluctable investiture, that engenders a rancorous and ferocious response. A rich and respectable tradition already exhorts us, if we wish to plumb the soul's depth, to work back from virtue to the hidden processes that produce it, to strip the great moral principles of their a priori character, to unseat obligation, that absolute pretender: to unveil, in a word, *the nonmoral secret of morality*. The categorical imperative, from this perspective, is a secondary process, derived from envy, aggressivity, or fear: an internalization. The child internalizes parental authority; sovereign power internalizes the castigations of resentment, recognizes its mistakes, and turns against itself. Lévinas answers these genealogies of morality with a reflection on Evil that divulges *the moral secret of immorality:* it is because I, in a fit of passion, as it were, cannot get away from an Other who always escapes me, because I am not my neighbor's equal but his chosen one, his hostage, his debtor, that aggressive drives overwhelm me at times.

"World Wars (and local ones), national socialism, Stalinism (and even de-Stalinization), concentration camps, gas chambers, nuclear arsenals, terrorism and unemployment—that's a lot for a single generation, even if it did nothing more than witness."[10] A widespread belief argues that to comprehend this enormity, we must relinquish love of neighbor as a pious but illusory idea. The opposite is in fact the case: thought, if it wishes to understand barbarism's enigma, must wrestle with this intrigue that ties us to our neighbor, one that we call by the worn name *love*.

HATRED OF THE OTHER MAN

Otherwise Than Being, or Beyond Essence is dedicated "to the memory of those who were closest among the six million murdered by the national-socialists, and of the millions on millions of all confessions and all nations, victims of the same hatred of the other man, of the same anti-semitism."[11]

At first glance, this dedication seems to place Lévinas in the intellectual mainstream, where hostility toward difference is seen as the cause of all the world's evils. Hatred of the other man: today, we call it *ethnocentrism*. A group deems itself the pure form of the human race and denies this status to other members of the species, or accords them, when pressed, a lesser humanity. A particular region's way of life lays claims to the totality of being and invades it, branding anything in the world that resists its model as inferior or monstrous. Man, according to the critique of ethnocentrism, is wolflike toward *other* men. And a crucial definition it is: for instead of naming likeness as the first cause of aggression, it is difference, the unknown, the marginal, the man from elsewhere, the man whose odd ways disturb one's serene sense of feeling at home, a man whose disturbing foreignness menaces the quotidian. Originary violence is not the war of all and against all invoked by classical thought but is the hostility that a human community—whether family, village, nation, religion, or cultural entity—almost always harbors toward strangers: the spontaneous violence of the parochial spirit cleaving to its own, a violence of ideology and conquest originating in a trait that elevates itself to the status of universal law, that claims a monopoly on civilization, and that sets itself against human diversity instead of recognizing the equality of cultures. Joining with such hostility to difference are a narrow individualism and false universalism: together, they comprise the shadowy coalition that an entire movement of European thought—from Montaigne to Lévi-Strauss—opposes with the apologetics of cultural pluralism.

This critique of ethnocentrism reaches its peak in the 1960s with decolonization. The Third World liberation movement—waged by the Other, so long misunderstood, ridiculed, and trapped by the impossible alternatives of inferiority and assimilation—provokes Europe to a fundamental reconsideration of Western imperialism. European man believed himself to be civilization incarnate: what was not him could not be other but must simply be less worthy. This was a certainty destined for destruction: for behold Western man, now different himself, *an other among others,* in tenuous possession of a provisional identity. In order to fight, from within, this act of force by which a particular culture sought to impose its dominance over an entire universe, philosophy swears allegiance to ethnology and history and their two grand schemes. By confronting earlier periods or distant cultures, our present moment suffers a healthy humiliation and shifts its place in our contemporary scene. All that we had believed immortal or natural in man is recast as something in process. Aspects of human behavior that seemed ahistorical—emotion, instinct, or conscience—take on a different meaning according to the diverse contexts in which they play out. The famous death of man is nothing but universal man's dissemination into countless identities that follow one after another, mix together, or oppose another, but never coalesce into unity.

All that remains of "the great historico-transcendental

destiny of the Occident" in this tumultuous landscape is the arbitrary quality of an insatiable will to power.[12] But if we are constituted entirely by history or culture, if the universal is nothing but imperialism's mask, if nothing in "man is sufficiently stable to serve as the basis for self-recognition, or for understanding other men,"[13] then we can no longer be the judges of anything. Our judgments, in fact, tend to establish a continuity and resemblance between the diverse faces of man, like the trace of ethnocentrism in our thought. Our values themselves are historically or culturally produced, our moral categories a sign of our difference. Forgetting this means we have fallen back into imperialism by once again investing a particular system with an absolute and timeless sway.

By proclaiming ourselves to be the other, in order to be done with phobia toward the Other, as the structuralist generation urges us to do, we arrive at an insurmountable contradiction: a contradiction between this project's ethical inspiration (the critique of western ethnocentrism) and its goal (dissolving morality into a general relativism). No obligation can be of value to everyone in a world where an irreducible multitude of humanities proliferate, confront each other, and disappear.

Despite the similarities in vocabulary, Lévinas cannot be enrolled in this school of thought. He certainly does correct the adage *homo homini lupus* so it refers to hatred of the *other* man, but he simultaneously objects to the confusion of alterity and difference that lies at the heart of the ethnocentric thematic. It is not specific qualities or odd customs that bring about the Other's alterity but the nakedness of his face: a call to my responsibility and a refusal to allow itself to be wrapped in its own exoticism. The Other obligates us and escapes, and Nazi anti-Semitism is proof: there is no hatred more violent than one that assaults the indiscretion and liberty of the face.

The oldest injustice done the Jews, to be sure, targets their tenacious adherence to the moral life: an attitude of separation toward the rest of the world and the barriers they construct with apparent pleasure between themselves and the rest of humanity. Apparently, anti-Semitism has never forgiven the Jewish people this kind of stiff-necked separatism, which the Nazi madness tried to wipe from the earth. But take a look at texts such as *The Protocols of the Elders of Zion* and *Mein Kampf,* which prepared the way for the Holocaust. Their chief concern is Jewish invisibility: the occult power wielded by Jews and the underhanded manner in which Jews insinuate themselves into the healthy institutions of other countries in order to sap their blood, weaken them, and bring about their eventual demise. Jewish difference is a worrisome evil only because it cannot be pinpointed once and for all.

In the indictment that Hitlerism brought against the Jews, two charges predominate: parasitism and conspiracy. At times Zion is presented as a secret society and its members as clandestine operatives of an enemy power that infiltrates official institutions and runs the world from behind the scenes. Elsewhere the Jews are portrayed as harmful bacilli, vampires, spiders, or bloodsuckers who slowly feed on the blood of other peoples. Tentacular or parasitic, this anti-race bears no comparison to the animal. It deserves only the subanimal status of vermin or microbes. What these metaphors announce, beyond the infamy they spout, is that the Jew is not an inferior being but an intangible one. That he is at once everywhere and invisible. That he is other and indistinguishable. That he conspires and proliferates, without ever showing himself in the light of day. That phantom-like and omnipresent, he is *the intruder* who introduces infection to healthy societies; he is an *undetectable* presence who also escapes the gaze and thus the vengeance of his victims. Ah! If he were only different, what a relief for humanity! But his identity consists precisely in not being identifiable. The hatred of the Jew aims at this ontological betrayal, this constitutive statelessness, this infidelity to essence that leads him to produce nothing but a fleeting, conflicted, indeterminate identity that is impossible to fix in a specific region of being. Neither man nor beast, the Jew, properly speaking, is nothing. And this is the crime—having no role as a being except to destroy being with his unlocatable presence—for which the final solution, with its methodical delirium, would make him pay.

Of what are the Jews guilty? Everything, the Nazis reply. Natural catastrophes and financial crashes. Floods and unemployment. Poverty, wars, and the various abominations that cast humanity into disarray and deprive it of the happiness to which it aspires. By laying the totality of evil traits at the door of a single nation, the Nazis prove themselves faithful to the age-old tradition of the scapegoat. And by cleansing the world of Jewish pestilence, they mean to achieve the grand feat of purification. For them, the Jew is the providential culprit and the expiatory victim for all calamities, offering, above all, expiation for that essential disaster, that transcendental plague from which all else springs: the Other. "My freedom does not have the last word; I am not alone": [14] this is the scandal, the intolerable fact. By ridding the world of the Jews, the Nazis promised to annihilate the curse of alterity.

Their complaints were absurd, of course, just as the temptation to heap every evil afflicting man onto a single object was madness. But the mad truth of this delirium is that the Other effectively inhabits our existence as an intruder, and that he flees it like a thief; that our debt to him grows larger the more we pay it off, and that our wish to define his image once and for all is constantly frustrated. The other, in as

much as he is Other, produces a contradictory form of irri-
tation, presenting himself to us as both a weighty obligation
and an evanescent lightness escaping our grasp. An inexorable weight. An unbearable lightness. The truth of this delirium is finally that the Other, breaking in, uninvited, demands our love in tribute, without asking our opinion.
What is Nazism? The hatred of this unchosen love, the revolt
against this unequal bond, against this commitment which
precedes any contract, any conscious deliberation. *Gott mit
uns,* said the executioners, invoking God's will and the sacred
character of their earthly duty, with the sole purpose of doing away with *the call* of their neighbor. God is with us, and
so we owe nothing to anyone else; we are chosen, so our
liberty has the last word, instead of being invested, chosen
by the Other, that is to say converted into responsibility with
respect to him. This notion, *Gott mit uns,* like that of *sacred
territory* or *sacred egoism,* transcends all ideology: it carries
the dream of an absolute sovereignty to a paroxystic extreme
where it can roam untrammeled by any sense of obligation:
the metaphysically utopian dream of a world in which a being could spread his wings, creating his own shape, becoming himself—without ever bumping into the human. To be,
in effect, as someone still put it quite recently, the Other
must not be.[15]

Accusations of parasitism and conspiracy are groundless.
Aberrant though they may be, such accusations nonetheless
translate the essence of the Other's inaccessibility and hold
over me, the source of his prerogatives, into the language of
resentment (whether this "me" is understood or imagined
as an individual, a nation, or a race). The hatred of the other
man thus consists of more than a gesture of exclusion demanded by loyalty to the universal or by blind attachment
to local traditions. The wish for revenge of a fallen ego, seeking total power, also plays its part. The Other is a wound

from which anti-Semitism hopes to heal being and unburden the world.

THE ETHNIC NOSE

"The great challenge to the modern period, and its peculiar danger, has been that in it man for the first time confronted man without the protection of differing circumstances and conditions."[16] Following Tocqueville, Hannah Arendt here defines the modern age as the triumph of the principle of sameness. Modernity is "the equality of conditions": not the end of inequality but the perception of modernity as egalitarian. Privilege and disparities persist, of course, but are not converted into hierarchies that determine one's essence. Men are different: but this no longer means that there are multiple humanities. Gradations of status and the marks that separate individuals fall by the wayside, and qualities of similarity take the fore. The modern, democratic age insists on the intrinsic identity uniting man rather than on the concrete traits that divide him: a vision of representative man is set against the heterogeneity of behavior and roles. If, for example, the categories of ruler and ruled still persist, their worlds are no longer closed off from one another: they can no longer be defined as separate castes or groups, characterized by their own temperament or distinctive modes of insight. The prerogatives a group might enjoy, or the power that it is able to exert, no longer leads to the necessary conclusion of its natural superiority. Even while each plays its opposing role in the social sphere, master and servant recognize themselves in each other, instead of spontaneously recognizing the uncrossable boundary standing between them. Economic inequalities may very well get worse: symbolic inequality dissolves. The principle of resemblance takes its place at the heart of human relations.[17]

It is at just this moment—when the Other is approached anew, without the exoticism that defuses, distances, and fixes him—that his reality has the power to call me into question. For it is when I recognize him as someone like me that my debt to him begins. His face must be separable from his qualities, must transcend his specific attributes, for his injunction to affect me, for me to feel the burdensome weight of his existence. As long as the Other is locked into his difference, I escape his prayer, his call, his summons: I am, in other words, sheltered from his alterity. I owe him nothing. I can watch him, find him amusing, live near him, or even peacefully coexist with him. I owe him no debt, and my view of him in no way runs the risk of transforming itself into responsibility. My being itself is not affected by this encounter. The familiarity I so generously observe is nothing but the flip side of my complete insensitivity. Only when the mask of difference has been shattered is that undesirable and dizzying feeling born: obligation.

At what point do we *alienate* the mad in western societies? The moment their uniqueness no longer stands alone. When the oddities of their behavior and the fluctuations of their reason are no longer sufficient to allow them to sustain an irrevocably distinct character. Democratic attitudes free the mad from the difference that imprisoned them, for the first time making them disturbing to society and an encumbrance to it. This malaise and this responsibility give rise to the asylum, a compromise that balances our concern to control madness with our need to escape it. To worry about mental illness, that is, both to isolate it and to be concerned with it, to cure it, but from afar, to take on its burden and to defend against it: such is the bastard solution that imposes itself in the face of "a difference that, to man's great sorrow, we confusedly begin to realize does nothing to hinder the idea of identity based on affiliation."[18] Interning the mad means not the exclusion of madness but, on the contrary, its incorporation into the human community. As long as the insane were seen as absolutely different from people with reason, it was possible to live in proximity with them. The mad, idiots, and the sick had no place in European social life before the age of equality except one marked by "an uncrossable divide" between them and "ordinary mortals."[19] Once this split was healed, or obscured by the progress of democratic thought, coexistence was no longer an option: after being something other than man, the madman became another man. Ceasing to be a monster, he could no longer be put on display. His difference no longer conjured up his alterity, and his exotic anomaly no longer concealed the debt owed him by normal men. The Other peered out from behind the spectacle of lunacy, and the asylum bears witness to the modern age's ambivalent confrontation with this change.

Tocqueville believed that this "invincible march of equality" would mean a decrease in violence and an easing of harsh social mores. A century and two world wars later, the author of *The Origins of Totalitarianism* analyzes violence's response to the terrifying aspects of the direct encounter of man with the other man. Read Hannah Arendt's formulation once more: the crisis of difference constitutes not only the distinctive sign, she argues, but the unique danger of the modern age. The man emancipated from his background is more difficult to confront than the man who is defined by it. Why? Because suddenly, he has a face, and I, as a result, have a responsibility. My neighbor is my brother—he encumbers me the moment that nothing protects me from his humanity. He threatens to meet me on the same terms as everyone else, that is to say, as a creditor, unless I can continue to confine him to his status or role. This multifaceted menace to the security of being has provoked a counter-attack whose most *accomplished* (in all the meanings of the word) form was anti-Semitism.

"Everything seems impossible or frightfully difficult," Maurras declared, "without the providential gift of anti-Semitism. With it, everything falls into place, levels out and is simplified." With the Jew, in fact, modernity simultaneously finds its cause and its remedy. He is the one who sits patiently in the shadows, who eats away at hierarchical structures, who orchestrates their decline; he is the foil that permits them—imaginarily—to be reconstituted. The illness is diagnosed and cured in a single stroke: if our guideposts become blurred, if traditional society founders and comes face to face with uncertainty, it is the fault of the Jew and his crafty machinations. Thanks to the idea of the Jew, the test of proximity is removed, doubt vanishes, and the world can be divided into isolated regions, into heterogeneous species, into a hierarchical "us" that need not communicate with the rest. The Jew is the artisan of disorder, and the validation of the reason for creating the social order to come.

By revealing the man who is different to be a neighbor, and by continuously dissolving the demarcations between spheres of social existence, the modern age places individuals under a dual suspicion. They can no longer find respite from a social order that keeps them in their place and subjects them to its traditions; but neither can they trust the system to confine the Other with rules that regulate social intercourse and codify every aspect of interpersonal relations. Anti-Semitism gets rid of two distasteful conditions, killing two birds with a single stone: individual liberty and universal proximity.

The anti-Semite enjoys his life, with a clear conscience and with complete impunity. For what should he answer? His failings have been excused in advance. Anti-Semitism gives him membership in an elite group from which he can never be expelled, since he belongs to it through the privilege of instinct and heredity. Ancestral wisdom serves as an infallible guide for his every step. The mystique of rootedness protects him against pangs of doubt: all things considered, he need merely exist—or flourish, as we say of a plant—to manifest his genius and superior sensitivity in every way. His worth is eternally secure, and no accident, no misstep, can keep him from enjoying it.

As for those disowned by this aristocracy—Jews, or those who have been "jewified"—they levy no obligation upon the anti-Semite, except perhaps that of self-defense, since their humanity is a lie and their very proximity an unacceptable aggression. Take Barrès describing Captain Dreyfus on the day of his humiliation: "As he came toward us with his cap thrust down over his forehead, his pince-nez on his ethnic nose, his eyes dry and furious, his whole face hard and defiant, he cried out, no, he ordered in his unbearable voice: 'You must tell all of France that I am innocent.' "[20]

The ceremony has just concluded: Dreyfus's clothes are in shreds; his saber has been broken; the gold braids from his cap and sleeves, the red stripes from his trousers, and his epaulets have all been ripped from his uniform and thrown to the ground. Dreyfus is nothing more than a man without decorations, without rank, without qualities. And at this moment when he is stripped of all ornament, reduced to this essential nudity, and demanding justice, Barrès gets worked up over his voice, his nose—that guilty protuberance—over the expression on his face. Frantically, he dresses Dreyfus in racial characteristics to escape being summoned, to punish Dreyfus for the humanity that the nakedness of his face seeks to arouse. The ancient aversion to Jews culminates here in a revolt against the social bond. In Dreyfus, it is not difference that Barrès abhors but proximity: the isolation and misery that calls to him in "an unbearable voice." This is why Barrès so vehemently imprisons Dreyfus in his difference.

Before it becomes intolerance of diversity, hatred of the other man (and anti-Semitism furnishes the model) displays the self's intolerance in the face of its own responsibility.

THE SWALLOWED-UP FACE

Thus the paradox becomes clear, and the contradiction is erased between "a life dominated by the presentiment and the memory of the Nazi horror"[21] and an *oeuvre* that rejects any special claim to insight when it dares to argue the notion that man is his own neighbor. For the Nazi horror constitutes precisely the most methodical and demented effort yet made to put an end to this unbearable proximity.

What does the idea of neighbor really mean? That a solidarity exists between one person and another, "a more ancient commitment than any decision that can be remembered."[22] That the other man—even before he is identifiable, and whatever his origin or his qualities—communicates, in all his defenseless nakedness and absolute weakness, the commandment "Thou shalt not kill." In this, we recognize the profound inspiration of the democratic revolution. And if the national socialists, after first having tested out their exterminatory methods on the mentally ill, later undertook the liquidation of the Gypsies and the Jews, peoples without armies, without lands, without states, peoples deprived of the arms that other nations usually bear, it was not just a matter of unleashing fury or frustration on the most feeble elements of the subjugated masses. National socialist hatred exceeded the bounds of its own Machiavellian logic. Their enmity was toward the neighbor as such, directed against this weakness that is an assault on life, that summons life to justify itself and forbids it exercise of its assertive strength; toward a poverty that puts force to shame, an impotence that robs force of the right to appropriate, seize, subjugate, and give itself free reign. It was therefore necessary to wage a merciless war in a fight to the death with weakness so that Hitler's dream of "a hard, violent and cruel youth, with the strength and the beauty of young wild beasts" might come to pass.

The Nazis offer double proof of this powerful form of weakness, both in their frenzied anti-Semitism and in the bureaucratic apathy with which they took up annihilation's work. In the radicality of their project and the banality of its execution. In the irrationality of their discourse and in their coldly rational methods. In the senseless rage of their ideology and in the meticulous zeal of their functionaries. This archaic insanity of the word and this ultramodern technological performance are nonetheless based in a single desire: to abolish the neighbor, to erase him *by* murder, to punish him for his face, and to erase him *from* the act of murder in order to escape his face at the critical moment when he is being killed.

How did they do it? How, at Auschwitz, Chlemno, Treblinka, Belzec, Sobibor, and Maidanek, did the unimaginable become commonplace? Through what miracle were those in charge of the final solution, mostly good fathers and husbands, able to turn genocide into an ordinary part of their lives and to participate in the slaughter of millions and millions of men, without any feeling of human affinity? Here is the answer that journalist Gitta Sereny received from Franz Stangl, commandant of Sobibor between March and September 1942 and of Treblinka between September 1942 and August 1943.

You see . . . I rarely saw them as individuals. It was always a huge mass. I sometimes stood on the wall and saw them in the tube. But — how can I explain it — they were naked, packed together, being driven with whips. [23]

Sereny concludes: "It became clear that as soon as the people were in the undressing barracks—that is, as soon as they were naked—they were no longer human beings for him. What he was 'avoiding at any price' was witnessing the transition."[24]

Such is the miraculous effect of heaping people together, the miracle of nude bodies: a universe materializes in which all men are interchangeable, homogeneous, identical. *Strip them* and *group them:* this two-faceted action that appears to be wholly functional in fact deprives the person of the mysterious privilege his face confers. What existed as a unique, irreplaceable reality is degraded to the level of an infinitely reproducible specimen or example. What was once capable of causing shame, of inhibiting the murderous impulse, and of turning spontaneity into bad conscience is now little more than a bit of nondescript flesh. Bound together and naked, whether in a concentration camp, on a nudist beach, or on the stage of an avant-garde theater, in the depths of servitude or the apogee of liberty, men lose at once the specificity that distinguishes them from one another and the resemblance that brings them together: neither similar nor different, they are the *same,* anticipating the radical identity to which they will be reduced by death.

This simple act of concentrating flesh in a single place causes all boundaries to disappear; nothing is delimited: the individual drowns in the mass, and the face no longer stands out from the rest of the body. The human shape is compressed and presents itself as a single continuous piece: the continuity, broken by clothing, between the body and the nakedness of the face, is reestablished. And what is more: the body takes over the face, turns its own nudity, as it were, into a kind of dress. If the body is naked, the face is not; or rather, it becomes naked in the same way. Part of the same fleshy entity, the face extends the body's nudity all the way to the hairline. The mass becomes a collective body that devours individuality; the body becomes an organic mass that consumes the face.

Thus the ss strips the clothes from those they are preparing to kill in order to hide their identity. Beyond any instrumental reason that might be invoked to explain the disrobing of people about to be gassed, their method seeks to mask the person as a moral entity by means of physical presence and thus to forestall a confrontation of the executioners with the face. *Incorporated* twice over, forceably inscribed in their own body and in the mass they form with the others who stand condemned, the victims are annihilated even before they die, and their murder will only serve to verify the status of "already dead" with which their lives will henceforth be confused. Nothing remains of the other, put in a pile and covered by the "shroud"[25] of his nudity: no soul, no individuality, no transcendence, no sanctuary whatsoever. His inner resources can no longer pose any obstacle to his own destruction. The naked mass wins out over inviolability.[26]

Like Hess at Auschwitz, like Eichmann in his offices in Berlin, like those numberless technocrats of extermination who worked at every level, Franz Stangl *concentrated on his work*. Thanks to a system of destruction that—and here is the magic of the technique—avoided the face of the victims, he succeeded in forgetting murder from within murder itself: genocide became a routine apocalypse, a sector of activity among others, freed of the elements of its own reality, a law of productivity, an activity concerned above all with bettering its performance, with beating its own records. Abstract murder, we might say, in the way Marx spoke of abstract labor to designate that moment when work (as something specific to the individual) ceases to be confused with the individual and becomes independent of the multiple forms he can take.

The indifference to the particular kind of labor corresponds to a form of society in which individuals pass with ease from one kind of work to another, which makes it immaterial to them what kind of work may fall to their share.[27]

With Nazism, this principle of indifference, literally un-leashed, spread everywhere until it reached the realm the Nazis considered the most basic: hatred of the other man. Barbarism itself became a job, if only because the contact between assassins and their victims was minimized, and be-cause the victims were never able to appear as persons, *with faces the world could see.*

The Nazis, in other words, understood how to get rid of confrontation with the face everywhere, and rid it from the final solution's most graphic scenes. Their logic demanded that two applications be carried to their extremes: *surveil-lance,* which would make itself invisible, thereby transform-ing "the whole social body into a field of perception,"[28] and *abstraction,* which allows escape from the presence and gaze of the very subjects over whom total power is held. On the one hand, they kept the concentration camp prisoners in "a conscious and permanent state of visibility"[29]; on the other, they numbered the prisoners, and then, at the moment of execution, they herded the victims together and stripped them naked, in order to render them *indistinct* from one another, to deprive them of their human form. In this way, the Nazis established a sphere of total administration: a dual power that controlled human beings while turning away from them; a gaze without a face, and a force without con-frontation. We know that bureaucracy frees human inter-actions from the risks of direct relationship, and those scru-ples to which proximity can give rise. Nazism completed this emancipation by turning mass murder into a bureaucratic affair.

The Test of the Neighbor

Franz Stangl was not permitted everything: for him, the confines of the camps were not a fantasy realm where prohibitions were violated, or where inhibitions fell away. No aggressive exuberance in his behavior. He was nothing like a sadist and would never have thought of accomplishing such an arduous task by relying on the savagery of his instincts alone. He was not permitted everything, but with the faces of his victims neutralized, everything was possible. Everything—which is to say, going beyond the bounds of Evil when it is a function of rage, heeding only bestial impulses. Everything—meaning the invention of a conscientious mode of living without conscience, applying the standards of productivity to the destruction of men, appreciating genocide in terms of production, fusing murder and administrative or industrial work into a single practice. It is only in a world without a face that absolute nihilism can establish its law.

6

Who Is the Other?

When I encounter the other man face to face, instead of working side by side on a common task, his face lays claim to me. When mediation ceases to temper our relation, when his role, status, or the particular traits that delimit him no longer protect me from his presence, when he reveals himself to me *point blank,* the Other controls me with his weakness, immediately turning me into his debtor. With unbelievable presumption, he asks me to be for him, before I am for myself. He seems to subject himself to my power, but in his surrender it is I who is torn from my repose, burdened, and called into question. The more he is at my mercy, the more I am summoned to his aid. "[T]he face of the neighbor obsesses me with this destitution. 'He is looking at me'—everything in him looks at me; nothing is indifferent to me."[1]

Hatred is one of the possible responses to this call, a hatred that consists of far more than instinctual selfishness or the denial of difference. Aversion toward the other man is proportionate to the debt incurred toward him: infinite and inexpiable. This is what is to be learned from the Nazis, however little we might wish to examine them, as something more than an episode in history: as one revelation of human potential.

But let us take a final look at Germana Stefanini, the part-time guard at Rebbibia prison, and her trial at the hands of Red Brigade terrorists. Did Stefanini try to mount any defense? Did she break down in sobs? Did she flee into stupefaction? "You don't move us," her judges replied, espying the confession that lurked beneath the mask of her silence or awkward apologies. Before their power executes her, their knowledge takes hold of Stefanini: they have decided on her oppressor status in advance, just as Dreyfus's guilt, for Barrès, was determined by his background. Dreyfus was destined to commit treason, if only by his "ethnic nose": his guilt was obvious, as obvious as the nose on his face. Both of these parties, the mad heirs of communism and those minor precursors of the Nazi scourge, break all social bonds between themselves and their enemies, even judicial ones, in favor of the supposed insight into those enemies they possess. Even if both share a common practice, if what we are witnessing in both cases is the destruction of the social by pseudoknowledge (what we have earlier called *stupidity*), the motives in each diverge radically.

While Barrès describes justice as "the force that develops with no other rule than itself" and the Nazis eliminate anything that stands in the way of expanding their being, Stefanini's judges place their being in the service of the proletariat, the poor, and those deprived of everything and seeking recompense. The first group wants to be able to say "We" without any hindering scruple placed on the unfolding of their essential power. To sustain an unchallenged sense of being, they destroy within themselves the weakness of being for others in order to become like a raging torrent or a self-generating power.[2] The second group, on the contrary, sacrifice themselves—with complete sincerity—for the weak and the lost. They kill not the Other but *for the Other,* out of loyalty to their ethnic destiny, not in open revolt against a responsibility they have not chosen as their own.

Unlike Barrès, who declared, "I revolt if the law is not the law of my race," they commit murder not to shake off morality's yoke but out of a sense of moral obligation. In their struggle against exploitation and market society, they seek not to rid themselves of duty toward their neighbor but rather to honor it to the utmost, to prolong it in effective generosity. In their eyes, Germana Stefanini's death sentence was justified by the suffering of the lowly and the plight of the impoverished and the hungry. In the name of the widow and the orphan, they set upon a helpless woman. These terrorists counted themselves among the combatants. But what turned them to armed struggle or, more accurately, what gives them the illusion of waging war while they are killing a defenseless being is not the lust for power but the desire to bring justice to millions whom an unjust system confines to poverty. They feel conscripted, chosen, inspired by the damned of the earth. As protectors of their suffering brothers, they would give the last measure of their devotion. Stefanini cannot move them because they know who she is, a rigid knowledge dictated by their solidarity with the victims of oppression. This villainous murder is their way of serving the people, of appearing before the impoverished, of responding concretely to their call. In the name of higher compassion, they hide from emotion. Fraternity with those who have nothing leads them to eliminate Stefanini from the human community.

You cannot move us: we are too close to the oppressed to grant you the title of neighbor; we love the unfortunate too much to be sensitive to your distress, to let any connection with you, however fleeting, disturb the unshakeable certainty of our understanding of who you are. Love protects us from love. Devotion preserves us from the hazards of the social bond.

Siding with exploitation's victims once and for all, in each and every circumstance, is thus not a sufficient safeguard against the totalitarian temptation. Abel's camp can be just as murderous as Cain's violence. Poor Germana Stefanini takes her place beside millions upon millions of human beings, of every class and persuasion, who have fallen victim to the same love of the other man.

Well before Lenin and his various progeny, Robespierre was the first to have grounded terror in love for the unfortunate. "We sympathize with the oppressor," he declared, "because we are heartless toward the oppressed." Out of kindness toward suffering humanity, he therefore sought *to place compassion on a new footing,* proving himself a pitiless foe of every traitor or enemy who conspired against it, starting with the foremost oppressor, that enemy of the people par excellence: Louis Capet, the sixteenth of that name. A simple deputy from the Montagne at the moment when the convention takes up the delicate question of a "trial for Louis XVI," Robespierre immediately proposes the most hard-line position. The king must not be *judged* but executed straight away.

To suggest that Louis XVI be tried, in whatever manner, is to take a step backward toward royal and constitutional despotism; it is a counterrevolutionary idea, for it puts the Revolution itself into litigation. In fact, if Louis can still be the object of a trial, he can be absolved; he can be innocent. What am I saying! He is presumed innocent until proven guilty: but if Louis is absolved, if Louis can be presumed innocent, what becomes of the Revolution?[3]

The Revolution deposed the king and proclaimed the people sovereign. To judge Louis now, to set up a tribunal, to consider testimony, to observe painstakingly the rules of penal procedure, to provide this accused the guarantees promised to all citizens by a regime that has just brought down tyranny and arbitrary rule: in the name of justice, such a procedure would contest the legitimacy of the issue up for adjudication. The scrupulous exercise of legal procedure would result in a shameful debate on the legitimacy of revolutionary justice. The scandal of the affair was precisely that: those in favor of a trial wanted to travel back in time, to fight the march of history, to distinguish the victims from the perpetrators, as if the people, while casting off their chains, had not already settled this question.

The right to punish the tyrant and the right to dethrone him are one and the same; the forms implied by one are the same as those of the other. Insurrection is the tyrant's trial; the judgment, the fall of his power; his penalty, whatever the liberty of the people demands.[4]

The Revolution strikes at the enemies of the people; justice claims to account for their crimes and to determine their legal fate. Thus, a fissure opens up, exposing a contradiction between revolutionary and judicial procedures. It is either time to judge or time to punish. Either—and such is the Revolution—the verdict of the people against their oppressors must be carried out on the spot, or the verdict is yet to come, and no decisive event has brought crime and tyranny to an end. In a word, either the Revolution has proclaimed the king guilty, or the guilt of the king remains a problem, and a tribunal exists where the verdict of the people can be appealed.

Two centuries later, the Red Brigades apply Robespierre's principle to Germana Stefanini. They interrogate her after condemning her because their religion is fixed: her true face has been recognized ahead of time, and they know to which camp she belongs. The only questions asked her are those to which they already know the answers. Instead of looking straight at Germana Stefanini the person, they penetrate her personality with their gaze, perceiving its function: behind her obvious weakness lies the power of a pitiless system. Judging Stefanini, considering the question of her guilt, would be to presume her innocence, to forget the suffering of "the imprisoned communist proletariat," and ultimately to place the Revolution's legitimacy on trial. By taking responsibility for human misery with their compassionate zeal, the terrorists free themselves of any and all obligation toward the accused they have forced to appear: the individual's trial thus amounts to nothing but a solemn preparation for an execution.

The comparison between Louis Capet and Germana Stefanini may seem an improper and shocking one. As the enemy of the people par excellence, Louis was the very incarnation the *Ancien Régime* and had conspired efficiently against the Revolution. In the guise of oppressor, Stefanini distributed packages to prisoners in an Italian prison. According to Robespierre's vision, killing the king reinforces the break with the old world and lends support to the changes taking place; killing Germana Stefanini did nothing to destabilize capitalism. The same love of the other man is unleashed on the despot and the feeble alike, denying them, for the same reasons, the guarantees of due process.

From 1793 forward, Condorcet takes to task the violence bred of this compassionate zeal. For it is not just those nostalgic for monarchy and its return who find repugnant Robespierre's thesis on the execution's legal validity. "The last of the philosophers of the great eighteenth century"[5] fiercely opposed it as well, finding himself to be the first among the revolutionaries to dare advocating the establishment of the republic after the king's flight.

In a case in which an entire offended nation is at once accuser and judge, it is to the opinion of humankind, of posterity, that such a nation must answer. It must be able to say: all the principles of jurisprudence recognized by enlightened men of all countries have been respected. It must be able to defy even the most blind partiality to cite any maxim of equity that has not been observed.[6]

In other words, not only does the king deserve to be judged, but his trial must be an exemplary one, "safeguarding even the smallest requirements of justice." This is the condition justifying the new regime's dismissal of the old, the condition that would have turned 1789 into a truly founding event. By deposing Louis XVI, the Revolution hoped to substitute the rule of law for the absolutism of the prince. By not judging him or by judging him hastily, the Revolution would betray its meaning and would prove, in a certain way, that nothing had really changed. "To assassinate without prior instruction those whom public outcry had judged,"[7] as Robespierre repeatedly demanded, would mean a return to despotism, *falling back* into barbarism, having finished with the king, to be sure, but allowing the regime he represented to stand intact.

For Robespierre, it is the execution of Capet that turns the Revolution into regicide; for Condorcet, it is the trial. Two definitions of revolutionary struggle face off here, revealing their fundamental incompatibility for the first time. In one, law takes its stand against arbitrary judgment; in the other, the people stand up to their enemies, and the rights of man are no longer sacred when, to triumph, the people find it necessary to suspend them.

The convention sides neither with Condorcet's juridical position nor with the maximalist camp of Robespierre. The king is tried, but by the representatives of the people themselves, in spite of Condorcet's fears that a single party might become "at once accuser, judge and defendant," and that the vote of the members of the convention would take place by show of hands, when according to the tribunal imagined by the encyclopedist, "the law would accord the accused the right of challenging jury selection, and the judges would agree to a secret vote."

But the Terror that takes hold several months later turns the debate in Robespierre's favor. Concern for the oppressed wipes out every hindrance and subterfuge the law places in its way. The creation of the Revolutionary Tribunal sets up a peremptory, inflexible process. With public accusations given unquestioned power, there are no defenders for those who have conspired against the fatherland, no witnesses to determine whether material or moral evidence exists independent of the oral testimony. The law's liquidation out of love for the less fortunate is complete. Compassion has once again found its proper object: it no longer spends energy on Cain that should more properly be used on Abel's behalf. And nothing, no formal juridical procedure, comes between the enemies of the people and the terrible punishment reserved for them by those who seek to aid the miserable.

The People: this utterance is, as Hannah Arendt notes, the key word to the French Revolution. It designates at once the part and the whole, the plebeians and the collectivity in its entirety. To the latter, the Revolution would return sovereignty. The Enlightenment *philosophes* had already proclaimed that princely authority comes not from God but from the people, meaning all the citizens. The revolutionaries added that the people must henceforth exercise the power of which they are the only legitimate source. A power, it is true, that is restrained by all rights held by the individual, which it is expressly enjoined to respect and to guarantee. It is by being *both* constitutional *and* democratic that the Revolution tries to do away with the capital sins of absolutism: the government of one man and of limitless power.

This was no doubt enough to satisfy the citizens, who, killing two birds with one stone, reclaimed their rights and took a share—by virtue of the vote's sanction, at least—of power. But the plebeians? Those *unfortunate people,* "the immense and laboring class whom pride awards this illustrious name with its hoped-for undertone of scorn?"[8] Do they ask for nothing more? Will their suffering bring them to accept treatment according to the same rules followed by those whose opulence brought it to pass? Is it justice, in other words, to handle the executioners and their victims alike? Sincere supporters of the people reply: no. Procedural safeguards enrage them, and so does a justice that deliberates rather than devastates, that renders judgments instead of casting thunderbolts. They are enraged by a justice that, in a world *whose verdict is already in,* still insists on deliberating when virtue demands punishment and nothing else.[9] What ails the plebeians, as Marx would later say, is a suffering that is universal and a wrong that is absolute. What final piece of evidence does the case against oppression require for the oppressors to be punished? *The justness of their cause is a given:* equivocation of any kind is a sign of a despicable plot to save supporters of despotism from the people's anger and a government of liberty. "No," writes Edgar Quinet, *republican* historian of the nineteenth century, "the system of the Terror was not a necessary result of the times but of faulty ideas."[10] Faulty ideas born of fanatical love: it was compassionate zeal and devotion to the plebeians that deprived the people as a whole of the rights that the Revolution had torn free for them. "Indulgence for the royalists? Mercy for the villains? Never! Mercy for innocent, mercy for the weak, mercy for the unfortunate! Mercy for humanity!"[11]

The ambiguity embodied in the term *people* reveals two competing conceptions of democracy that have divided modernity since the French Revolution. In the first of these conceptions, *people,* used pejoratively and restrictively by the ruling class to refer to those of low extraction, expands until it encompasses all those who belong to the city, without exception. Inequality of status is no bar to membership, and there is but a single humanity, a single people—even if it is composed of several distinct or antagonistic social groups. In the other conception, these disparities win out over proximity, and status inequality once again serves as a bar to belonging. Two humanities come into being: the plebeians and their enemies. Not everyone belongs to the people: still, the people are everything, a "shackled and oppressed everything," in Siéyès's words, shackled and oppressed by an order of privilege that conspires to do them harm. And what are Condorcet and his friends seeking when they demand a trial with due process for this leader's conspiracy? What does their legalism mean? Why are they so determined to reopen a closed case, to raise the question of Louis XVI's guilt once more, or to reconsider whether he should be punished? They are trying to save the tyrant; they have become royalty's defenders: they ask for due process for partisan reasons, or such is the certain conviction Robespierre holds. While appearing to respect the rule of law, they use juridical quibbles and time-wasting tricks to hobble the administration of justice. You cannot sit as judge and at the same time be party to the complaint, Condorcet proclaims. You can only be a party, Robespierre retorts. In the constant battle between the people and their enemies, there is no place for a neutral stance. Impartiality is an imposture, and any reference to a universal rule of law is nothing but a way of weakening popular justice to benefit a fiction of process. The legalism that the Marxists will call bourgeois is a night in which all the cats are gray: the strongest and the weakest, the capitalists and the workers, the prison guards and the prisoners—in a word, those given to prejudice and those on whom it is inflicted. The conflicts are resolved only after they are transposed into a world where their meaning evaporates. Juridical equality masks social inequality and brings about new violence, which it claims to fight.

According to this logic, one is either for the oppressed or for the oppressors, for a sclerotic social order or for humanity, but one cannot, under any circumstances, claim to split the difference. In the battle between the plebeians and their enemies, each side acts from *partisan* concerns, and no one is *impartial*. It is thus law itself that is brought before the tribunal of compassionate zeal, and law that is condemned for the double crime of hypocrisy and obstruction of justice.

CONDORCET'S OMELET

What is goodwill? It is the response "here I am" when one is hailed by a face: "Here I am under your gaze, under obligation to you, your servant."[12] It is the feeling of being called into question by the voice speaking to you—obligated, accused, conscripted—and the acceptance of this exorbitant responsibility. Rather than bristling or turning away, it is the act of welcoming one's neighbor in bad conscience, which is to say the very model of moral hospitality. We can speak of goodwill when a being "suspends [his] spontaneous movement of existing,"[13] forgets his own being in order to make the being of another his concern. An occurrence all too rare these days, it is often said, thus forgetting that many acts performed out of guilt or bad conscience are no less threatening to humanity than the refusal of responsibility. Evil—not merely criminal but malicious—is brought about by representatives of goodwill at least as frequently as it is caused by those who stand for cruelty. And the "here I am," in recent history, has accomplished devastation equal in intensity and horror to the devastation wrought by those who take responsibility only for "me and mine."

Goodwill inflects my relations with my neighbor, out of fear of him. Yes, but who is my neighbor? We are not two. Immediately there appears a third "other than the neighbor, but also another neighbor." Thus the question springs to mind: "What have they done to one another? Which passes before the other?"[14] To which face should I devote myself? The elan of "here I am" must be modulated, compared, measured, judged, reflected upon. The face binds man to goodwill, but goodwill itself is bound to thought by the multiplicity of faces: "Earthly morality invites us on a difficult detour that leads to third parties, outside of love."[15]

Unless you wish to wreak terrible havoc, do not try to confront existence armed with this adage alone: "Love, and do what you wish." Nothing is more malleable than unreflecting goodwill; and nothing is more terroristic than goodwill grounded in hard and fast knowledge, based on an absolutist thought, which claims to have worked out the problem of the Other once and for all. The former perspective does not deliberate but responds, with indefatigable alacrity, to the calls that are addressed it, thereby giving full usage of itself to the devil as well as to God. The second perspective has deliberated and does nothing more than put its moral conclusions into practice. For unreflective goodwill, there is no problem: its "here I am" is unconditional and immediate. For compassionate zeal, there is *no longer* any problem: it has reduced the multiplicity of faces to two and invested its ardor in the service of the plebeians. The Other is none other than the people. To judge the king, to judge *tout court,* would mean that the Incorruptible had denied this fundamental precept and set a scandalous insensitivity against misery's overwhelming proof.

"The way leads from responsibility to problems"[16]—such is, however, the path. Love of neighbor does not lead to justice except by keeping open the question of the Other;

such love leads to terror when it believes the question has been resolved.

Condorcet is the victim of this dogmatic goodwill, after having been its opponent. When a warrant for his arrest is issued 8 July 1793 for protesting against the constitution adopted by the members of the convention, he hides out in the home of the widow of the painter Horace Vernet, who, in her house on the Rue des Fossoyeurs, near Luxembourg, "took in several boarders."[17] There, the outlawed *philosophe* composes *L'Esquisse pour un tableau des progrès de l'esprit humain,* seeking, Michelet tells us, to "terrify the Terror with the triumphant powers of Reason."[18] Having finished this work and refusing to compromise his hostess any longer, Condorcet makes his way, on foot, to Fontenay-aux-Roses and the home of friends: yet they dare not show him any hospitality. Condorcet wanders a full night and day in the country. His strength exhausted, he enters a cabaret in Clamart where he orders an omelet of several eggs, paying with a gold piece. In his pocket rests an edition of Horace. No detail is a trifle in times of social unrest. Everything has meaning. Eggs in rich excess, the gold piece, a volume of Latin poems—everything points to the vagabond's aristocratic origins. The Terror, connected for better or worse to the Enlightenment *philosophes,* is not the Enlightenment's apotheosis but its negation. Those we call the *philosophes* revered knowledge and fought against what they called *obscurantism:* all the forces opposed to the independent transmission and dissemination of knowledge. They possessed, in Grimm's phrase, "the fury of the dictionary," which is to say the will to destroy superstition by amassing and propagating learning. The Terror broke with this surge and replaced it with a new obscurantism: knowledge was despised, not because it violated dogma, but because it did not originate with the people. Now, it was not disobedience that was condemned but instead elitism and idleness. Reading Horace is certainly no sacrilege; unproductive and pretentious, it certifies the pride and laziness of its reader and his scorn for the common. Culture, for the *sans-culottes,* was no longer considered a universal value but was now an insult to equality, an obscene mark of distinction. With the Terror, the fallen, enlightened man ceases to be an example for other men and becomes suspect: "The peasants who were drinking there (they were the revolutionary committee of Clamart) saw straightaway that he was an enemy of the Republic."[19]

The committee had probably never heard of the author of *Essai sur le calcul intégral.* But its members, as backward as they might be, possessed a keen sociological eye and knew how to pick out a nonplebeian. These *modern* inquisitors would have condemned Galileo not for the substance of his discoveries but for the "aristocratism" of his white hands and the civic disinterest of his erudition. To serve the people, in their view, was to identify and denounce all the members of Cain's tribe who had infiltrated Abel's, all the parasites and the privileged hiding in the new egalitarian world. Condorcet was thus arrested and transferred to the prison of Bourgla-Reine. After a night of detention, he was discovered dead in his cell. Legend has it that he was poisoned, thus sparing the Republic "the shame of parricide, the crime of striking down the last of the *philosophes* without whom it would never have existed."[20]

The moral of this story (like the destiny of Germana Stefanini) is that morality itself needs to take systematic precautions against its own hubris and impatience. Social justice can be achieved only at the cost of those privileges that seek to sustain themselves through indifference toward their victims, and by giving up the popular justice that speaks in the name of the universal victim and culminates in an inevitable lynching. Love conjures up a world in the Other's weakness, in his face, in his oneness, a world always on the verge of being overwhelmed by the frigid waters of egotistical calculation or by the pure and simple administration of human masses. But this love of the other man also demands a subtlety and concern for truth that recognizes the necessity of calculation, limiting it to "the sober study of problems that are constantly renewed"[21]: so that we are constantly reminded that alterity has no owner, that its cause is never fully understood, and that the question "who is my neighbor?" can never be answered in abstract or definitive terms. As if in addition to the commandment to love our neighbor, imposed by his countenance, we were impelled to pursue the philosopher's task: that is to say, in a kind of etymological reversal, *to impart wisdom to love;* to resist, by the continual exercise of reason, the temptation to give a unique and immutable face to the other man. "In the proximity of the other, all the others than the other obsess me, and already this obsession cries out for justice, demands measure and knowing, is consciousness."[22]

If, as Flaubert's phrase has it, stupidity consists of wanting to come to conclusions, it is because we never get a certain fix on the Other that we can neither locate him nor define him. As amorous passion teaches us, the Other takes us beyond our previous constructions; and as conscience teaches love, there can be no profit in confiscating the name of neighbor.

THE WARM MONSTER

The State, "the coldest of all cold monsters" (Nietzsche), is usually held to account as the great perpetrator of terror. Set against democratic societies, which are still capable of protecting individuals from ravenous Big Brother, are totalitarian societies, which, as their name indicates, tend toward the total State. To contain the State: such would be liberty's grandiose and fragile venture. But in that part of the world where terror is law, the barriers have been reversed, and the sprawling State has spread over every social surface, leaving the individual neither retreat nor escape. We could not live happily or even tranquilly except in limited States, *hand-cuffed* States, and only the completely unhindered State deserves the name *totalitarian*.

"The State has become an idol that demands the sacrifice of the individual and nation," Franz Rosenzweig pronounced during this century's first decade. Premonitory words? Less so, perhaps, than those of Michelet, now speaking of Robespierre: "He conceives of the people as something other than the natural and reasonable vessel of eternal justice, but he seems to confuse them with justice itself. *Senseless deification of the people who subjugate the law to themselves.*"[23]

Throughout the nineteenth century, republican historians pondered the terrorist turn taken by the French Revolution and the risks of dictatorship inherent to democracy. For them, it is not the State as such that put an end to democracy, but the notion that all rights are ceded to the State at the moment the masses seize power. To enlighten a republic without terror, it became necessary to reconcile the people's claim to sovereignty with the need to protect civil liberties under the umbrella of state power. The State had to simultaneously emanate from the people and guarantee the rights of the individuals against all abuses, including those that the will of the people might commit. As Ledru-Rollin puts it: "Each and every usurpation of these rights would be a crime of outrage against humanity, and if the entire populace, minus one, were in cahoots, this would be an assault against social order, against principle, against the doctrine of sovereignty, for either a slave or a martyr would be created."[24]

The restitution of power to the people and the refusal to justify the arbitrary, even if the people are guilty of it: the republican idea came from this double demand and emerged just as much from a refutation of the revolutionary process as it did from a will to see it through.

Thus the "poor nineteenth century" offers more insight into the totalitarian phenomenon than contemporary invective hurled against the State.[25] For today, from Libya to Russia, popular tyranny has passed from the scene. Even as it was being perfected, the model of 1793 had moved on: taking the people as its point of reference and slogan, elevating the collective will above basic liberties, power rips up constitutions, alienates inalienable rights, smothers social relations under the blanket of gigantic bureaucracy, and introduces terror. To put it bluntly: totalitarianism arises from idolizing the people, not from idolizing the State.

Nowadays, this claim meets with almost universal agreement: in totalitarian regimes, whatever their stripe, the poor are oppressed in the name of the meek. Hallowed in word, the plebeians are, in fact, placed under surveillance, and by dint of the need to separate the wheat from the chaff, *the people seem to be composed of nothing but their own enemies*. It is not enough, however, to decry the gap between oppression's reality and the dithyrambic language of praise, or to denounce the creativity of populist beginnings that turn into a police state. For it is the people's sanctification that gives rise to despotism: the dithyramb leads to oppression, and fervor to bureaucracy. Love is not the mask behind which the criminal hides in order to deflect suspicion, but is rather the very motive of the crime. Terror's effective beginnings rest in the notion that all is permitted to the people: since legitimacy springs from them, all that is popular is legitimate. "Eternal sophism of the plebeians that they can, at their will, create absolutism; that this arm, in their hands, wounds no one; that it is, for them, Achilles' spear; that tyranny, if they exercise it, immediately sheds its evil character and becomes a good deed."[26] Totalitarian violence flows from this sophism and this confusion; its usurpation (taking the place of the people) and enslavement (prohibiting any action against the people) are paradoxically grounded in adulation (the people can do anything).

The people as opposed to the State, solidarity as opposed to deliberation: whether fascist or communist, such is the totalitarian program. For the former, it is a question of bending legal institutions to affirm the national will; the latter seeks to substitute the party of the oppressed for the State and to found a "civilization without rights" (Zinoviev) in the name of the rights of the weakest. In order to obliterate the right to security, the protection of domestic peace, civil liberties—in other words, both the functions and the limits of sovereign power according to classical legal theory—fascists invoke the dynamic power and primitive ardor of the masses. The people they describe and celebrate are identified with life's progressive principle—a people who embody the brilliant essence of organic spontaneity, salubrious instinct before it is tainted by intelligence, strength before scruples have labeled its capabilities guilty, animal vigor before it is made to account for its actions or to justify its impulses. The people as a natural community that existed before modernity's decline: "The people have revealed to me the human substance, and better yet, the creative energy, the earth's lifeblood, the unconscious."[27]

As heirs to the Jacobin terror, the communists lay their own claim to the universal suffering of the proletariat. They castigate, to use Marx's expression, "the absolute wrong" done to the worker by his status as wage earner.[28] What do the people want first? To seize control, to subjugate, to dominate—in short, to claim power. What do they want second?

To achieve justice for the damage inflicted upon them, for their exploitation as the greater part of humanity, and thus to save the world. And so we discover these two opposing camps (which nonetheless end up perpetrating the same violence): the people as a vital force that nothing must constrain (Hitler: "what is right is what is good for the German people"), martyrs who rise up against their executioners, in sheer will to power and in the holy will to reparation, revolting against love and the fixation on love, a being who aspires to self-fulfillment; and the Other who, having but one face, must be obeyed without question.

The Dreyfus affair brings these two motifs together for the first time. Dreyfus was guilty because he was a Jew, according to Barrès, who exalted the popular will against him and who hated him as Other. Guesde and Viviani denied Dreyfus victim status because he was rich and because they did not want to waste their compassionate energies on a person of privilege. To them, the importance accorded the affair was suspect: "They wouldn't make such a fuss if he were poor." In the eyes of the author of *Culte du Moi*, Dreyfus embodied the essence of the foreigner. For those socialists who reproached Jaurès for wanting to lead them into dubious battle, the foreigner was the proletariat: Dreyfus, as an officer and a bourgeois, was in no way fit to bear such a mantle. Not the principles he claims as his own—honor, country, uniform—nor his career, nor the place of origin, nor the places he visits—nothing about Dreyfus's person or personal history made him the archetypal victim: he is "excluded from the consideration that should be due a man without resources."[29] And so Dreyfus became the focus of prejudicial hatred as well as love. Condemned as Other or in the name of the Other, he is not of the people and makes a poor figure of a martyr. He is even subject to attack by his defenders, who judge him unworthy of his destiny. It is precisely because of this difference between the symbol and the face, between the struggle for the unfortunate and the persecuted man, between the man presumed to be Other and the actual Other, that Dreyfus is a hero of our times, and the affair itself "an inexhaustible subject of reflection."[30]

Prison guard Germana Stefanini, Captain Dreyfus, and the Encyclopedist Condorcet are the victims of two forms of fanaticism that offer man the chance to desert the human in the people's name. Obliged by the neighbor's face, committed to fulfill a responsibility he has not chosen, man is compelled to a perpetual questioning by the plurality of faces, by what Lévinas calls "the entry of the third party, a permanent entry, into the intimacy of the face to face."[31] A double burden overwhelms him, composed of obligation and deliberation. His life is at once ethical and problematic, disillusioned with the self because of the neighbor and disillusioned with the neighbor because of all the others. The people's victim status puts an end to the problem (the Other is known, once and for all), and the people as vital force absolves him of responsibility (everyone other than the people is treated as enemy). Deified egotism proclaims its fundamental aspiration: the wish to free itself from love. The need to treat the working class as holy affirms love's wish to free itself from wisdom. And it is because wisdom and love are not games but unwished-for vocations, heavy burdens to bear, that humanity oscillates between the two extremes of a morality without deliberation and an imperialism without morality.

Notes

INTRODUCTION

1. Alain Finkielkraut, *The Defeat of the Mind*, a new translation and introduction by Judith Friedlander (New York: Columbia University Press, 1994). For a different view and an excellent introduction to Finkielkraut, see Alice Y. Kaplan's introduction to Alain Finkielkraut, *Remembering in Vain: The Klaus Barbie Trial and Crimes against Humanity,* trans. Roxanne Lapidus with Sima Godfrey (New York: Columbia University Press, 1993).

2. See Arthur Schlesinger Jr., *The Disuniting of America* (New York: Norton, 1992), esp. chapter 4, "The Decomposition of America," 101–21. Neoconservatives historically supported American liberalism and the ethnic assimilation it demanded. Today, this assimilationist liberalism often results in hostility toward minority groups' demands for cultural inclusion. Many neoconservative intellectuals, moreover, began far to the left, like many of the "New York Intellectuals," shifting from communism and socialism to liberalism, and shifting as well to support for a cultural conservatism that marks the Right in the culture wars of today. For a history of this process before the culture wars proper began, see Alan Wald, *The New York Intellectuals: The Rise and Decline of the Anti-Stalinist Left from the 1930s to the 1980s* (Chapel Hill: University of North Carolina Press, 1987).

3. W. E. B. Du Bois, *The Souls of Black Folk* (New York: Bantam Books, 1989), 29.

4. Finkielkraut tells the story of his break with the Marxist tradition with autobiographical eloquence in *The Imaginary Jew,* trans. Kevin O'Neill and David Suchoff, introduction by David Suchoff (Lincoln: University of Nebraska Press, 1994).

5. For a relatively measured view of this position, see Robert Hughes, *Culture of Complaint: The Fraying of America* (New York: Oxford University Press, 1993).

6. See "Toward a Multicultural Society?" and "We Are the World, We Are the Children," in Alain Finkielkraut, *The Defeat of the Mind*, 87–135.

7. Alain Finkielkraut, "Conférence," speech delivered at the Prix Européen de l'Essai Charles Veillon (Bussigny, France: Fondation Charles Veillon, 1984).

8. See Alain Finkielkraut, "La sainte alliance des clergés," *Le Monde*, 25 October 1989, 2 [our translation], and Elisabeth Badinter, Régis Debray, Alain Finkielkraut, Elisabeth de Fontenay, and Catherine Kintzler, "Profs, ne capitulons pas!" *Le Nouvel Observateur*, 2–8 November 1989, 58–59.

9. For a different perspective on Finkielkraut's view of the Enlightenment, see Alain Finkielkraut, "Universalisme et liberté de l'esprit," *Les Nouveaux Cahiers* 85 (summer 1986), 28–30.

10. See Gilroy's exploration of black-Jewish cultural tensions, "Children of Israel or Children of the Pharaohs," and "Black Culture and Ineffable Terror," in Paul Gilroy, *Black Atlantic: Modernity and Double Consciousness* (Cambridge: Harvard University Press, 1993), 205–23, and his comments on Lévinas in particular (p. 213).

11. For a useful account of these connections, see Simon Critchley, *The Ethics of Deconstruction: Derrida and Lévinas* (Oxford: Blackwell, 1992); for Derrida's own tribute to and critique of Lévinas, see Jacques Derrida, "Violence and Metaphysics: An Essay on the Thought of Emmanuel Lévinas," in Jacques Derrida, *Writing and Difference,* trans., with an introduction and additional notes, by Alan Bass (Chicago: University of Chicago Press, 1978).

12. In making this universal claim for the right to cultural difference, Finkielkraut fits well into a strong tradition of Central European Jewish thought, represented by figures as diverse as Franz Rosenzweig, Walter Benjamin, Martin Buber, Hermann Cohen, and Hermann Levin Goldschmidt. For another, contemporary account of this position, see David Suchoff, "Widersprüchliche Identität: Judentum und Postmoderne im Werk Hermann Levin Goldschmidts," in Willi Goetschel, ed., *Perspektiven der Dialogik* (Vienna: Passagen Verlag, 1994), 111–24.

13. See Judith Friedlander, "The Lithuanian Jewish Enlightenment in French Translation: Emmanuel Lévinas and His Disciple Alain

Finkielkraut," in her *Vilna on the Seine: Jewish Intellectuals in France since 1968* (New Haven: Yale University Press, 1968), 80–106. Lévinas, born in Lithuania in 1906, died in Paris on 25 December 1995. See obituary by Peter Steinfels, "Emmanuel Levinas, 90, French Ethical Philosopher," *New York Times,* 27 December 1995, Section B, 6.

14. Robbins's treatment of this issue shapes her review essay, "An Inscribed Responsibility: Lévinas's *Difficult Freedom,*" MLN 106 (1991), 1052–62, which provides a fine general introduction to the two sides of Lévinas's work. Robert Gibbs makes the same point more extensively, placing Lévinas in postmodern thought as well as the Central European Jewish tradition, in his *Correlations in Rosenzweig and Lévinas* (Princeton NJ: Princeton University Press, 1992).

15. George Steiner, "Lévinas," *Cross Currents,* 106 (summer 1991), 245.

16. Elsewhere, Finkielkraut has discussed the Dreyfus case exemplary of the role of the public intellectual in modernity, which he sees as lacking in the postmodern age. See Alain Finkielkraut, *Le Mécontemporain: Peguy, lecteur du monde moderne* (Paris: Gallimard, 1991).

17. For a similar application of the liberal concept of citizenship to multicultural approaches to literary studies, see John Brenkman, "Multiculturalism and Criticism," in Susan Gubar and Jonathan Kamholtz, eds., *English Inside and Out: The Places of Literary Criticism* (New York: Routledge, 1993), 87–101.

18. "Languages are not strangers to one another," Benjamin wrote, "but are, a priori and apart from all historical relationships, interrelated in what they want to express." See Walter Benjamin, "The Task of the Translator," in his *Illuminations,* trans. Harry Zohn (New York: Schocken Books, 1969), 72. On the relations between Benjamin's and Lévinas's use of Jewish sources, see Susan Handelman, *Fragments of Redemption: Jewish Thought and Literary Theory in Benjamin, Scholem, and Lévinas* (Bloomington: Indiana University Press, 1991).

19. See Charles Taylor, "The Politics of Recognition," in his *Multiculturalism and the "Politics of Recognition"* (Princeton NJ: Princeton University Press, 1992), 72.

20. See "Ethics and the Face" and "Reason and the Face," in Emmanuel Lévinas, *Totality and Infinity: An Essay on Exteriority,* trans. Alphonso Lingis (Pittsburgh: Duquesne University Press, 1969), 197–204, here p. 202.

1. THE ENCOUNTER WITH THE OTHER

1. Cf. Alexandre Kojève, *Introduction to the Reading of Hegel,* trans. James H. Nichols Jr. (New York: Basic Books, 1969), 33.

2. Emmanuel Lévinas, *Time and the Other,* trans. Richard A. Cohen (Pittsburgh: Duquesne University Press, 1987), 34.

3. Emmanuel Lévinas, *Existence and Existents,* trans. Alphonso Lingis (The Hague: Martinus Nijhoff, 1978), 29.

4. Emmanuel Lévinas, "L'Existentialisme, l'angoisse et la mort," in *Exercices de la patience,* no. 3/4 (1982), 26 [trans. O'Neill and Suchoff].

5. Lévinas, *Existence and Existents,* 84.

6. Jean-Paul Sartre, *Being and Nothingness,* trans. Hazel E. Barnes (New York: Philosophical Library, 1956), 254.

7. Sartre, *Being and Nothingness,* 364.

8. Sartre, *Being and Nothingness,* 364.

9. Sartre, *Being and Nothingness,* 390.

10. Emmanuel Lévinas, *En découvrant l'existence avec Husserl et Heidegger* (Paris: Vrin, 1974), 23 [trans. O'Neill and Suchoff].

11. Lévinas, *En découvrant l'existence,* 178 [trans. O'Neill and Suchoff].

12. Emmanuel Lévinas, *Difficult Freedom,* trans. Sean Hand (Baltimore: Johns Hopkins University Press, 1990), 9.

13. Emmanuel Lévinas, *Totality and Infinity,* 50–51.

14. Lévinas, *En découvrant l'existence,* 125 [trans. O'Neill and Suchoff].

15. Lévinas, *Difficult Freedom.*

16. Emmanuel Lévinas, *Autrement qu'être ou au-delà de l'essence* (The Hague: Martinus Nijhoff, 1978), 67. [trans. O'Neill and Suchoff].

17. Emmanuel Lévinas, *Humanisme de l'autre homme* (Paris: Fata Morgana, 1972), 49. [trans. O'Neill and Suchoff].

18. Lévinas, *Totality and Infinity,* 215.

19. Lévinas, *Humanisme de l'autre homme,* 15. [trans. O'Neill and Suchoff].

20. Roland Barthes, *Roland Barthes,* trans. Richard Howard (New York: Hill and Wang, 1977), 169.

21. Emmanuel Lévinas, *Otherwise Than Being or Beyond Essence,* trans. Alphoñso Lingis (The Hague: Martinus Nijhoff, 1981), 124.

22. Lévinas, *Otherwise Than Being,* 120.

23. Lévinas, *Difficult Freedom,* 18.

24. Lévinas, *Humanisme de l'autre homme,* 81 [trans. O'Neill and Suchoff].

25. Lévinas, *Otherwise Than Being,* 11.

26. Maurice Blanchot, *The Unavowable Community,* trans. Pierre Joris (New York: Station Hill Press, 1988), 44.

27. Henry James, *The Beast in the Jungle* (New York: A. M. Kelley, 1937), 79.

28. Henry James, *The Notebooks of Henry James* (New York: Oxford University Press, 1947), 311.

29. James, *The Beast in the Jungle,* 124.

2. THE BELOVED FACE

1. Emmanuel Berl, *Sylvia* (Paris: Gallimard, 1972), 126 [trans. O'Neill and Suchoff].

2. Berl, 112 [trans. O'Neill and Suchoff].

3. Berl, 111 [trans. O'Neill and Suchoff].

4. Berl, 131 [trans. O'Neill and Suchoff].

5. Lévinas, *Otherwise Than Being,* 120.

6. Marcel Proust, *Remembrance of Things Past,* 3 vols., trans. C. K. Scott Moncrieff and Terence Kilmartin (New York: Random House, 1981), 2:160.

7. Proust, *Remembrance of Things Past,* 2:161.

8. Proust, *Remembrance of Things Past,* 2:158.

9. Proust, *Remembrance of Things Past,* 2:162.

10. Henri Bergson, *Laughter: An Essay on the Meaning of the Comic* (London: Macmillan, 1913), 185.

11. Bergson, *Laughter,* 185.
12. Proust, *Remembrance of Things Past,* 2:164.
13. Proust, *Remembrance of Things Past,* 1:528.
14. Proust, *Remembrance of Things Past,* 1:528.
15. Roland Barthes, *A Lover's Discourse,* trans. Richard Howard (New York: Hill and Wang, 1978), 83.
16. Proust, *Remembrance of Things Past,* 1:318.
17. Barthes, *A Lover's Discourse,* 113.
18. Lévinas, *En découvrant l'existence,* 230 [trans. O'Neill and Suchoff].
19. Lévinas, *Totality and Infinity,* 257.
20. Proust, *Remembrance of Things Past,* 1:851–52.
21. Proust, *Remembrance of Things Past,* 3:65.
22. Proust, *Remembrance of Things Past,* 3:64.
23. The phrase "together, but not yet" (*ensemble mais pas encore*) is taken from Maurice Blanchot's *L'Attente, l'oubli* and from the commentary preceding Emmanuel Lévinas's *Sur Maurice Blanchot,* (Montpellier: Fata Morgana, 1975), 38 [trans. O'Neill and Suchoff].
24. Lévinas, *Time and the Other,* 36.
25. Proust, *Remembrance of Things Past,* 1:955.
26. Derrida, *Writing and Difference,* 103.
27. Proust, *Remembrance of Things Past,* 1:956.
28. Lévinas, *Ethique et infini: Dialogues avec Philippe Némo* (Paris: Fayard, 1982), 69 [trans. O'Neill and Suchoff].
29. Proust, *Remembrance of Things Past,* 1:396.
30. Lévinas, *Otherwise Than Being,* 11.
31. "Despite the difficulties of my story, despite discomforts, doubts, despairs, despite impulses to be done with it, I unceasingly affirm love, within myself, as a value." Barthes, *A Lover's Discourse,* 22.
32. Proust, *Remembrance of Things Past,* 3:930.
33. Spoken by Ysé in Paul Claudel, *Partage de midi* (Paris: Gallimard, 1949), 143 [trans. O'Neill and Suchoff].
34. Paul Claudel, *Le Soulier de Satin* (Paris: Gallimard, 1982), 270 [trans. O'Neill and Suchoff].
35. Lévinas, *Time and the Other,* 89.
36. Georges Bataille, *Erotism,* trans. Mary Dalwood (San Francisco: City Lights Books, 1986), 17. Or again on page 19: "What we

desire is to bring into a world founded on discontinuity all the continuity such a world can sustain."

37. Lévinas, *Totality and Infinity,* 260.

38. Proust, *Remembrance of Things Past,* 1:396.

39. Lévinas, *Totality and Infinity,* 295.

40. Lévinas, "L'Autre dans Proust," in *Noms propres* (Montpellier: Fata Morgana, 1976), 155–56 [trans. O'Neill and Suchoff].

3. FACE AND TRUE FACE

1. Roland Barthes, *A Lover's Discourse,* 22.

2. Gustave Flaubert, *Madame Bovary: Life in a Country Town,* trans. Gerard Hopkins (Oxford: Oxford University Press, 1981), 72–73.

3. Trans. note: in this chapter, where Finkielkraut quotes Sartre, it seems no accident that he places Flaubert's Homais among the representatives of modern times (*Les Temps Modernes*), which is the title of the famous journal founded by Sartre a century later.

4. Jean-Paul Sartre, *The Family Idiot,* 4 vols. trans. Carol Cosman (Chicago: University of Chicago Press, 1981–93), 1:623.

5. Sartre, *The Family Idiot,* 1:622.

6. Louis Martinez, "La 'langue de bois' soviétique," in *Commentaire* 16, 515 [trans. O'Neill and Suchoff].

7. Lévinas, *Difficult Freedom,* 207.

8. Jean-Claude Milner, *Les Noms indistincts* (Paris: Seuil, 1983), 134 [trans. O'Neill and Suchoff].

9. Flaubert, *Madame Bovary,* 106.

10. Flaubert, *Madame Bovary,* 107.

11. Robert Musil, "De la bêtise," in *Essais* (Paris: Seuil, 1984), 315 [trans. O'Neill and Suchoff].

12. From an article by Marcelle Padovani, *Le Nouvel Observateur,* 3 June 1983 [trans. O'Neill and Suchoff].

13. Albert Camus, *The Rebel: An Essay on Man in Revolt,* trans. Anthony Bower (New York: Alfred Knopf, 1967), 3.

14. Cited in Jean-Denis Bredin, *L'Affaire* (Paris, Julliard, 1983), 235 [trans. O'Neill and Suchoff]. We chose not to use the standard translation, *The Affair: The Case of Alfred Dreyfus,* trans. Jeffrey Mehlman (New York: G. Braziller, 1986).

15. Cited in Jean-Denis Bredin, *The Affair: The Case of Alfred Dreyfus,* trans. Jeffrey Mehlman (New York: G. Braziller, 1986), 251.

16. Maurice Barrès, *La Terre des morts,* cited in Raoul Girardet, *Le Nationalisme français* (Paris: Seuil, 1983), 187 [trans. O'Neill and Suchoff].

17. Barrès cited in Girardet, *Le Nationalisme français,* 186 (trans. O'Neill and Suchoff).

18. Francis Ponge, *The Voice of Things,* trans. Beth Archer (New York: McGraw Hill, 1972).

19. Elias Canetti, *Crowds and Power,* trans. Carol Stewart (New York: Viking Press, 1962), 375.

4. BREAKING THE WORLD'S SPELL

1. A journalistic variant of this philosophy: it is society that is speaking through you; therefore, you are said to be interesting. A French daily of large circulation (*Libération*) was sued for having published a letter in its letters to the editor section, during the Israeli siege of Beiruit, that called for the murder of the Jews of France. Many comrades were outraged at this recourse to the legal system: Was this unleashing of hatred symtomatic? Did it possess an inestimable documentary value? Must we avert our eyes in the face of social violence, while making our appeal to the law's archaic violence? The call for murder laid bare a particular state of affairs, and this alone justified its publication. Because everything is revelatory, everything is permitted, and because no word is free, there ought to be no limits placed on freedom of expression. In the name of freedom, justice was accused of still believing that men are free enough to respond to answer for what they say.

2. "Men such as Saint-Juste and Robespierre had a particular vision of justice coming suddenly to the earth. They believed themselves to have touched upon this ideal. They imagined themselves as only a few heads away. In comparison with such an infinite good that beckons so close, what are a few heads stubbornly opposed to the entire human race? Nothing." Edgar Quinet, *La Révolution* (Paris: Imprimerie nationale), 2:130.

3. Lévinas, *Totality and Infinity,* 79.

4. Lévinas, *Difficult Freedom,* 54.

5. Lévinas, *Difficult Freedom,* 14.

6. Lévinas, *Difficult Freedom,* 15.

7. Lévinas, *Difficult Freedom,* 15–16.

8. Franz Rosenzweig, *The Star of Redemption,* trans. William W. Hallo (New York: Holt, Rinehart and Winston, 1970), 171.

9. Lévinas, *Totality and Infinity,* 54.

10. Lévinas, *Totality and Infinity,* 58.

11. Lévinas, *Nine Talmudic Readings,* trans. Annette Aronowicz (Bloomington: Indiana University Press, 1990), 152. This disqualification of the word to the profit of the hidden discourse that murmurs within, without the speaker's knowledge, opens onto what Michel Foucault calls one of the major contradictions of our moral life: "Everything postulated as a human truth owes a debt to irresponsibility." Michel Foucault, *Historie de la folie à l'age classique* (Paris: Gallimard, 1961), 475 [trans. O'Neill and Suchoff].

12. Maurice Blanchot, *The Infinite Conversation,* trans. Susan Hanson (Minneapolis: University of Minnesota Press, 1993), 127.

13. Lévinas, *Difficult Freedom,* 232.

14. Moses Maimonides, *The Guide for the Perplexed,* trans. M. Friedlander (London: George Routledge and Sons, 1936), 86. In the same spirit, Lévinas writes that these attributes *thematicize* what tradition simply calls The Name: "In so doing they get nearer to God as though to an essence which then distances them from the unrepresentable and holy, that is, absolute God, who is beyond all thematization and all essence." Emmanuel Lévinas, *Beyond the Verse: Talmudic Readings and Lectures* (Bloomington: Indiana University Press, 1994), 120.

15. Jean-Paul Sartre, *Notebook for an Ethics,* trans. David Pellauer (Chicago: University of Chicago Press, 1992), 34.

16. Lévinas, *Totality and Infinity,* 58.

17. Lévinas, *Totality and Infinity,* 78.

18. Guy Petitdemange, "Éthique et transcendance, sur les chemins d'Emmanuel Lévinas," in *Recherches de sciences religieuses,* January–March 1976, 66 [trans. O'Neill and Suchoff].

19. I here make use of Lévinas's account in "La Souffrance inutile," in *Giornale di metafisica,* Genoa, 1982.

20. Maimonides, *The Guide for the Perplexed*, 86.
21. Lévinas, *Difficult Freedom*, 280.
22. Maurice Merleau-Ponty, *Humanism and Terror*, trans. John O'Neil (Boston: Beacon Press, 1969), 153.
23. Ian Patocka, *Essais hérétiques* (Paris: Verdier, 1982), 144 [trans. O'Neill and Suchoff].
24. Elias Canetti, *Crowds and Power*, 282.

5. THE TEST OF THE NEIGHBOR

1. Lévinas, *Totality and Infinity*, 104–5.
2. "Creation posits a being outside the self in such a way that he is able to exist without the constant support of his creature . . . the act of creation is what brings something other than God into existence, another whose alterity is total." Catherine Chalier, *Judaïsme et altérité* (Paris: Verdier, 1982), 181–82 [trans. O'Neill and Suchoff].
3. Since its origins, psychoanalysis has been the stake in a battle between a philosophy of realism and a philosophy of liberation, between the critique of illusions that promise to put an end to human conflict and the critique of a system that keeps man from reaching this ideal state. In his own way, Freud continues to oppose the invariants of human nature to the utopia of a civilization delivered from evil. The precise reproach levied by an entire tradition—from Reich to Marcuse to Deleuze and Guattari—is that it sees only the social order as it stands in the psychological ordeals of contemporary man. "The Strength of Reich consists in having shown how psychic repression depended on social repression. Which in no way implies a confusion of the two concepts, since social repression needs psychic repression precisely in order to form docile subjects and to ensure the reproduction of the social formation, including its repressive structures. But social repression should not be understood by using as a starting point a familial repression coextensive with civilization—far from it; it is civilization that must be understood in terms of a social repression inherent to a given form of social production." Gilles Deleuze and Felix Guattari, *Anti-Oedipus: Capitalism and Schizophrenia*, trans. Robert Hurely, Mark Seem,

and Helen R. Lane (Minneapolis: University of Minnesota Press, 1983), 118.

4. Blaise Pascal, *Pensées,* no. 455, trans. W. F. Trotter (London: J. M. Dent and Sons, 1931).

5. Emmanuel Lévinas, *Otherwise Than Being,* 87.

6. Lévinas, *Humanisme de l'autre homme,* 75.

7. Lévinas, *De Dieu qui vient à l'idée* (Paris: Vrin, 1982), 145 [trans. O'Neill and Suchoff].

8. Lévinas, *De Dieu qui vient à l'idée,* 117–18.

9. Lévinas, *Otherwise Than Being,* 126.

10. Lévinas, *Noms propres,* 9 [trans. O'Neill and Suchoff].

11. Lévinas, *Otherwise Than Being,* vi.

12. Michel Foucault, *The Archaeology of Knowledge,* trans. A. M. Sheridan Smith (New York: Pantheon Books, 1972), 210.

13. Michel Foucault, "Nietzsche, Genealogy and History," in *Michel Foucault, Language, Counter-Memory, Practice: Selected Essays and Interviews,* ed. by Donald F. Fouchard, trans. Donald Bouchard and Sherry Simon (Ithaca, NY: Cornell University Press, 1977), 153.

14. Lévinas, *Totality and Infinity,* 101.

15. "What we Arabs want, is to *be.* We will only be able to be if the *other* is not." Ben Bella, *Revue de politique internationale,* 16 (1982), 108.

16. Hannah Arendt, *The Origins of Totalitarianism* (New York: Harcourt, Brace and World, 1951), 54.

17. On this subject, see François Furet, "Le Système conceptuel de 'la démocratie en Amérique,' " in *L'Atelier de l'histoire* (Paris: Flammarion, 1982), and Marcel Gauchet, "Tocqueville, l'Amérique et nous," in *Libre,* 7 (1980).

18. Gauchet, "Tocqueville," 92 [trans. O'Neill and Suchoff].

19. Gauchet, "Tocqueville," 91 [trans. O'Neill and Suchoff]. See also Marcel Gauchet and Gladys Swain, *La Pratique de l'esprit humain* (Paris: Gallimard, 1980).

20. Bredin, *The Affair,* 6.

21. Lévinas, *Difficult Freedom,* 291.

22. Lévinas, "Philosophie, justice et amour," in *Esprit,* August–September 1983, 16 [trans. O'Neill and Suchoff].

23. Gitta Sereny, *Into That Darkness* (New York: Vintage Books, 1983), 201.

24. Sereny, *Into That Darkness,* 203.
25. Milan Kundera, *The Book of Laughter and Forgetting,* trans. Michael Henry Heim (New York: Alfred A. Knopf, 1981), 226.
26. It is therefore not only offensive but also absurd to try to explain the functioning of the camps and the relations between their victims and executioners in terms of sexual perversion. With erotic nudity, the body of the Other becomes all face, and sexual relations become the experience of its inviolability. Nudity in the concentration camps has a goal that is quite rigorously the opposite: to absorb the face of the Other in its own body.
27. Karl Marx, *Contribution to the Critique of Political Economy,* trans. N. I. Stoke (Calcutta: Abinash Chandra Saha, 1904), 299.
28. Michel Foucault, *Discipline and Punishment,* trans. Alan Sheridan (New York: Pantheon Books, 1977), 214.
29. Foucault, *Discipline and Punishment,* 202.

6. WHO IS THE OTHER?

1. Lévinas, *Otherwise Than Being,* 93.
2. Cf. Jean Paul Sartre, *Anti-Semite and Jew,* trans. George J. Becker (New York: Schocken Books, 1948), 54: "The anti-Semite is a man who wishes to be a pitiless stone, a furious torrent, a devastating thunderbolt—anything except a man."
3. Robespierre, *Textes choisis* (Paris: Editions sociales, 1973), 72 [trans. O'Neill and Suchoff].
4. Robespierre, *Textes choisis,* 75 [trans. O'Neill and Suchoff].
5. Michelet, *Histoire de la Révolution française* (Paris: Laffont, 1979), 1:518.
6. Condorcet, cited in Dr. Robinet, *Condorcet, sa vie, son oeuvre* (Paris: Librairies-imprimeries réunies, 1893), 249 [trans. O'Neill and Suchoff].
7. Condorcet, cited in L. Cahen, *Condorcet et la Révolution française* (Paris: F. Alcan, 1904), 459 [trans. O'Neill and Suchoff].
8. Robespierre, cited in J.-L. Talmon, *Les Origines de la démocratie totalitaire* (Paris: Calmann-Lévy, 1966), 124 [trans. O'Neill and Suchoff].
9. "The people do not judge like courts of justice: they do not render judgments; they throw thunder." Robespierre, *Textes choisis,* 74 [trans. O'Neill and Suchoff].

10. Edgar Quinet, *La Révolution* 2:36 [trans. O'Neill and Suchoff].
11. Robespierre, cited in Talmen, *Les origines de la démocratie totalitaire,* 147 [trans. O'Neill and Suchoff].
12. Lévinas, *De Dieu qui vient à l'idée,* 123. [trans. O'Neill and Suchoff].
13. Lévinas, *Totality and Infinity,* 63.
14. Lévinas, *Otherwise Than Being,* 157.
15. Lévinas, "Le moi et la totalité, in *Revue de métaphysique et morale* 59 (1954), 361 [trans. O'Neill and Suchoff].
16. Lévinas, *Otherwise Than Being,* 161.
17. Michelet, *Histoire de la Révolution française,* 2:761. [trans. O'Neill and Suchoff].
18. Michelet, *Histoire de la Révolution française,* 2:762 [trans. O'Neill and Suchoff].
19. Michelet, *Histoire de la Révolution française,* 2:763 [trans. O'Neill and Suchoff].
20. Michelet, *Histoire de la Révolution française,* 2:764 [trans. O'Neill and Suchoff].
21. Georges Hansel, "Le Talmud, le folklore et le symbole," in *Colloque des intellectuels juifs de langue française: Israël, le judaïsme et l'Europe* (Paris: Gallimard, 1984), 98.
22. Lévinas, *Otherwise Than Being,* 158.
23. Michelet, *Histoire de la Révolution française,* 2:203 [trans. O'Neill and Suchoff].
24. Ledru-Rollin, *Du gouvernement direct du peuple,* cited in Claude Nicolet, *L'Idée républicaine en France* (Paris: Gallimard, 1982), 366 [trans. O'Neill and Suchoff].
25. For a critique of antistatism, see Blandine Barret-Kriegel, *L'État et les esclaves* (Paris: Calmann-Lévy, 1979).
26. Quinet, *La Révolution,* 2:111 [trans. O'Neill and Suchoff].
27. Barrès, "Le Jardin de Bérénice," in *Le Culte du Moi* (Paris: Plon, 1922), 350 [trans. O'Neill and Suchoff].
28. Cf. Jean-François Lyotard, *Tombeau de l'intellectuel et autres papiers* (Paris: Galilée, 1984), 19.
29. Blanchot, "Les Intellectuels en question," in *Le Débat,* 29 May 1984, 15 [trans. O'Neill and Suchoff].
30. Blanchot, "Les Intellectuels en question," 9 [trans. O'Neill and Suchoff].
31. Lévinas, *Otherwise Than Being,* 160.

Index